Rediscovering the Power of Repentance & Forgiveness

FINDING HEALING AND JUSTICE FOR RECONCILABLE AND IRRECONCILABLE WRONGS

Dr. Leah Coulter

Rediscovering the Power of Repentance & Forgiveness

FINDING HEALING AND JUSTICE FOR RECONCILABLE AND IRRECONCILABLE WRONGS

Dr. Leah Coulter

ampelōn
PUBLISHING

Atlanta, Georgia

Rediscovering the Power of Repentance & Forgiveness
Copyright ©2006 by Leah K. Coulter

ISBN: 0-9748825-9-3
Printed in the United States of America
Requests for information should be addressed to:
Ampelon Publishing
6920 Jimmy Carter Blvd., Ste. 200
Norcross, GA 30071

To order other Ampelon Publishing products, visit us on the web at:
www.ampelonpublishing.com

Cover & inside design: Lisa Dyches — cartwheelstudios.com

Printed on 10% post-consumer recycled paper

Dedication

*I dedicate this book to You, LORD. You have brought
me from a place of darkness into the light of Your grace
and righteousness because of Your incredible gift of
salvation and forgiveness. Thank You for opening my
heart and ears to the cries of the sinned-against.
I love You, LORD.*

*I also dedicate this book to my husband, Bill. You are my
greatest ally, friend, encourager, and partner in this work.
I love you, Bill.*

Acknowledgements

As I think about all the people God has brought into my life who have been instrumental in seeing this book come from a vision in my heart to the reality in your hands, I cannot help but acknowledge the following people:

My family, my students, and especially my brothers and sisters at the Channel Islands Vineyard who have encouraged me, dialogued with me, and prayed unceasingly for me in the writing phases of this book.

Jack Hayford, thank you for the example you are in my life and your encouragement in the writing of this book. Your Foreword deeply touched my heart and I value your support and friendship.

David Augsburger, Fuller Theological Seminary, thank you for helping to shape the practical theologian that I am today and for your kind endorsement.

Steve Robbins, founding pastor of Channel Islands Vineyard, thank you for seeing the academic gifting in me.

Dr. Paul Chappell, The King's College & Seminary, thank you for believing in me and encouraging me on to Ph.D. studies.

Jason Chatraw at Ampelon Publishing, thank you for understanding the necessity of this book at this time.

Angie Ramage, thank you for helping me refine this book through the editorial process. You made it quite enjoyable.

To the sinned-against that I have had the privilege to walk alongside, thank you for inviting me into your pain and allowing the Holy Spirit to counsel, teach, and transform us in the process.

To my husband, Bill, I enjoy wrestling through the Scriptures together and their practical applications. Thank you for your consistent love and encouragement and am very grateful to God that He has made us partners in the words and works of the Kingdom of God.

Table of Contents

Foreword

This is a book about forgiveness being "on earth as it is in heaven" (Matthew 6:10); a book that has its root in the ineffable source of the All-Powerful to forgive, but which points to the inescapable responsibility of our power when we repent. Decades of pastoral ministry have taught me the need for what is contained in these pages.

Fifty years of pastoring—of shepherding souls unto life, healing, God's wisdom, and heaven's hope—have involved innumerable conversations with good people seeking counsel. I have personally witnessed thousands who have stepped into the light of understanding the difference between "religious ideas" about God and a "relational revelation" from Him. These have verified God's grace to forgive and His power to transform any one of us, once our heart becomes touched as our mind is taught by His Spirit. And it is then—when heart and mind understand and receive the dynamic that flows from the cross of Christ, that the Spirit of God begets true repentance—that is, the turning of my mind toward alignment with God's, and the turning over of my will to yield to His. It is within this decisive encounter of any created being with the Creator of all, that human souls suddenly experience the magnanimity and majesty of forgiveness—of an unchaining from past guilt, folly, and self-centeredness, now replaced by a peace of mind and rest of the soul that only God can give.

Those foundational realities I have just summarized are the essential beginning place for all redemption—all forgiveness, all restoration of relationships, all recovering from brokenness—as the shame caused us either by ourselves or by others who violated us is removed. But from that foundational point, you will find this book crowding you forward nudging, goading you as it has me, with the inescapable implications of God's forgiveness lavished upon us. This "crowding forward" is not pushy, but you will find it purposeful. The writer is more interested in our well-being than she is in her thesis. You will find yourself caught up in the flow of clear thinking, driven by a purely motivated care and a sensitively-edged passion for a complete embrace of all the implications of God's forgiveness offers to and calls from us.

I have an acquaintance with Leah Coulter that spans over fifteen years. I'm familiar with the fruit of her life and the faithfulness of her and her husband's ministry. She has been sharpened by experience and mellowed by time, and you will sense something of her gentle graciousness as you read; a demeanor that enables our receptivity to what she presents as an unquestionably demanding issue. Matching her graciousness, however, you will find she is also patiently persistent as she points beyond the wonder of God's grace in forgiving us, to the workings of that grace that complete a cycle—so that all heavenside has achieved for us in Christ is not short-circuited by our failure to make the earthside connection through Christ.

One can hardly say enough about how practical and clear these pages are, so I welcome you to a profoundly human book, yet still one that is quite without the limits of mere humanism. You will also find it is a profoundly godly book, but without any of the trappings of pretentious piety. In all, Rediscovering the Power of Repentance and Forgiveness is something of a court summons intended to rectify injustices—perhaps ones that have been dealt to you. And since this court convenes in the presence of the universe's Judge, we will not be surprised to find perfect justice and equity, while discovering it is always administrated with loving kindness and gentle mercies. Only God as He is revealed in the Holy Bible is characterized by this incredible balance of unrelenting integrity to apply His law and overflowing fidelity to administer His love.

He wants to work that balance in each of us, not to enforce a law, but to release a grace. And as you read you, as I have, may find something deeper in His grace—something that will increase understanding, stir the wellsprings of your soul, and enrich your relationship with others. With that, it might well be that your will find this book personally therapeutic. But whether that is the case or not, I assure you of this—it will certainly increase your capacity to be a healing instrument of God's love in the midst of a very broken world.

Jack W. Hayford

Chancellor, The King's College and Seminary
Founding Pastor, The Church On The Way

Introduction

WHY ANOTHER BOOK ON REPENTANCE
AND FORGIVENESS?

Sitting with people in the ashes of their lives, struggling to find a way out of the pain and hurt in the aftermath of wrongs that have been done to them, gives you a unique perspective from within the world of a person who has been deeply wounded. From that vantage point, you quickly understand what it means to have been "sinned against" by other believers, family members, friends, neighbors, or strangers. Their voices have been muted, and they wonder if anyone hears their internal cries for justice. As you listen, you not only hear their voices, you begin to echo them—crying out to God with them, and asking Him to release them from the captivity and pain of those irreconcilable wrongs.

"How do I get out of here?" they want to know. "What does God want me to do?"

I realize forgiveness is a critical path that needs to be considered, but how often do we feel as though we must "sell" somebody on the idea of forgiving an unrepentant person for their own good, while reminding them that God won't forgive them if they don't forgive? Moreover, how do we deal with the unrepentant people who have hurt us—those who leave scars too deep for words?

From an all too common Christian view, why must the weight and responsibility of forgiveness be placed on the sinned-against instead of the sinner's repentance? During my years of study, I've heard two contradictory voices in Scripture regarding forgiveness. One admonishes us: "Forgive . . . anything against anyone" (Mark 11:25), while the other instructs us: "If another disciple sins, you must rebuke . . . and if there is repentance, you must forgive" (Luke 17:3).

13

I remember a time when I cried out to God for His wisdom to understand how forgiveness could bring justice. I also asked Him to provide a way out of the ashes for those trapped by the brokenness of life. "What is forgiveness all about, Lord? How do I reconcile the seemingly contradictory commands and the cries that I hear for justice?" This is when I realized God was answering my prayer. It was as if He had placed an answer within my heart, "It's in loving God and loving your neighbor."

As I started to recall the forgiveness Scripture passages that I had been studying, I began to see that some addressed forgiveness in our relationship with God, others addressed forgiveness in our relationships with other people, while still others talked about how we cannot separate these two dimensions. I began to rediscover forgiveness, seeing it from this whole new perspective—as a believer who lives in two relational dimensions, not one. My horizon or scope of knowledge regarding forgiveness had been expanded, and I began to understand the two differing voices regarding forgiveness. They are not contradictory at all, but indeed complementary, especially when understood from this two-dimensional worldview—providing clear paths for both the sinner and the sinned-against.

As you read these words, you may wonder, *Why another book on forgiveness?* The primary reason is because I believe biblical forgiveness and repentance must be linked and taught from this two-dimensional worldview. In *Rediscovering the Power of Repentance and Forgiveness*, I will freshly address this topic from a Judeo-Christian worldview, understanding that Jesus' teachings are rooted in Israel's Law. It lays the biblical foundation which teaches us that, in order to follow in the footsteps of Jesus, we must love God and our neighbor the way Christ loves us. This love is expressed in how we keep clean slates before God and other believers, non-believers, friends, coworkers, and even enemies.

Relational wounds can cut deeply and hinder our desire or ability to trust others and even God. Whether you're facing a broken relationship because of a sin you committed against another or are crying out for justice as the one sinned against, Scripture provides clear instructions in both dimensions of relationship. It is my prayer that the Holy Spirit will strengthen and encourage us to live our lives in true repentance and forgiveness—the kind of repentance and forgiveness that reconciles broken relationships, giving grace for the process of transformation, or provides a way to release those irreconcilable wrongs to our justice-making God—who will hold our offenders responsible. May the Holy Spirit continue to enlighten our hearts as we rediscover the power of biblical repentance and forgiveness together.

Leah Coulter, Ph.D.
Sr. Associate Pastor, Channel Islands Vineyard, Oxnard, CA
The King's College & Seminary Professor, Van Nuys, CA

one

The Missing Link in Forgiveness

W hen you think about forgiveness, what comes to mind? Do you find yourself remembering those times when you felt the heaviness of your heart lift because someone forgave you? Do you think back to a time when you felt pressed to forgive someone who never even repented or acknowledged the hurt and pain they caused you? However, you were told that forgiveness was what God wanted you to do for your own good. Or do you find yourself getting mad when you think about forgiveness because you have unresolved issues toward others you have hurt or who have hurt you? Are you afraid to ask God to forgive you because you have put off facing these issues? Are there situations in which your heart cries, "It's not fair to forgive them—they never said they were sorry or admitted their sin"? Or is there a time when the thought of forgiveness made you feel powerless against overwhelming pain and suffering?

I was teaching on the subject of forgiveness for the sinned-against—specifically men and women who had been sexually abused as children—when a Master of Divinity student kept raising his hand at the beginning of the lecture and making comments such as, "The Bible says they must forgive or they won't be forgiven." Every couple of minutes his hand would go up and he would ask another question or make another comment. I asked him to ride out the lecture with me, and to hold his questions until the end. Then I would explain why I believe Scripture teaches what it does regarding the subject of forgiveness, especially for irreconcilable wrongs.

This student was filtering what I was saying through his present and personal grid of understanding forgiveness. This is a natural thing to do. Whenever we receive new information, we process it through what we currently know. He agreed to hold his questions, and immediately after class, came up to me and said, "This was the best class I have had." At first, I didn't know if he was serious or what he meant.

The next week, he arrived early and asked if he could share something with the class. Cautiously, I asked, "What would you like to say?"

He said, "I went home after class and searched Scripture regarding forgiveness, and it does teach as you have taught in class." He continued by saying that he also tried to share his new understanding of forgiveness with his pastor. However, the pastor was in the exact spot he had been the week prior and contended, "No. People just have to forgive."

Not discouraged by his pastor's words, the student said, "I will win him over."

More importantly than this, he said, "I'm on staff at my church, and I've been counseling two different women who are working through sinned-against issues. Prior to this class, I told them they had to forgive their unrepentant offenders because God required it, and it would make them feel better. However, each of them was resistant because they felt this counsel was unfair and that God was unjust. I put into practice over the weekend what I learned last week. Both women not only understood this biblical model of forgiveness, but also embraced it willingly. They began to believe that God did truly care about their pain and losses, and were very willing to release their rights and the debts owed them by their offenders to our justice-making God."

He said he wanted to tell the class about his new understanding of forgiveness, and how it helped these two women experience a true release and freedom. He told his story to the class and said, "This information not only expanded my knowledge of forgiveness, but will also change the way I teach and counsel others regarding forgiveness issues." He had rediscovered the link between repentance and forgiveness and realized that they operate within two relational dimensions.

This student, like so many of us, previously understood forgiveness from a unilateral or one-dimensional viewpoint. In other words, he believed that forgiveness was something we did only in our relationship with God to make us feel better. "Just let it go. Forgive and you will feel better if you do."

However, Jesus taught that we must love God and love our neighbor (Matthew 22:34-40), thereby living in two relational dimensions: our vertical relationship with God and our horizontal or interpersonal relationships with others. Furthermore, these two dimensions are inseparable. How I live in relationship with other believers, nonbelievers, and even my enemies will affect my relationship with God. Conversely, my relationship with God must affect how I live in relationship with others.

Two voices are indeed heard in Scripture regarding repentance and forgiveness. One voice tells us: "Forgive . . . anything against anyone" (Mark 11:25), and another tells us: "If another disciple sins, you must rebuke the offender, and if there is repentance, you must forgive" (Luke 17:3). Trying to follow these commands from a unilateral viewpoint seems contradictory and confusing: "Do I let the offense go? Or do I go?" However, when understood from a two-dimensional viewpoint, these two Scripture verses give clear instructions for those who have been sinned against by others. Mark 11:25 prepares our hearts in our relationship with God, and Luke 17:3 moves our feet toward interpersonal reconciliation when and if the offender repents.

When we've sinned against others, Scripture is equally clear regarding our two dimensions of relationship: "Leave your gift there before the altar and go; first be reconciled to your brother or sister, and then come and offer your gift" (Matthew 5:23-24). We are commanded to repent and seek forgiveness from the one we've sinned against before asking God to forgive that sin. My willingness to go and be reconciled with the one I've offended is the first step in asking God to forgive me for that sin. In other words, the horizontal or interpersonal step towards reconciliation must take place, or at least be attempted, before I can be forgiven in my vertical relationship with God.

Repentance must be linked with forgiveness. How can we forgive and be reconciled with someone who has sinned against us and has never repented?

When we've been sinned against by others, Scriptures is equally clear regarding our two dimensions of relationship: "Forgive . . . anything against anyone" (Mark 11:25), and then: "If another disciple sins, you must rebuke the offender, and if there is repentance, you must forgive" (Luke 17:3). As we pray, we must have a willing heart to forgive our offenders whether we go and rebuke them for the sake of their repentance, or they are repenting to us—seeking forgiveness and reconciliation. Either way, our hearts must be willing to forgive.

We have been taught for years that we must forgive as the Lord forgives (Colossians 3:13). From a unilateral perspective, we have mistakenly believed that we must forgive people who have never repented to us and without ever confronting them. We have also been taught that when we've sinned against others, we only need to unilaterally ask God to forgive our sins without repenting to the ones we've sinned against. However, God does not forgive unrepentant sin. When we pray, repent, and seek His forgiveness, He graciously forgives, but not without requiring our repentance.

To "forgive as the Lord forgives" means that our love must be extended to those who have sinned against us, inviting repentance. Repentance must be linked with forgiveness. How can we forgive and be reconciled with someone who has sinned against us and has never repented? Maybe, he or she even refuses to repent. God doesn't even do that! Unless that person repents, there can be no forgiveness or reconciliation in the horizontal dimension. Instead, there is only a brokenness that deepens with time. Furthermore, unless we repent to those we have sinned against before asking God to forgive us for that sin, our prayers may not only be hindered, but we may also be confronted several times for the sake of our repentance.

In Matthew 18:15-20, we learn the steps to confronting another believer, and what to do if that person refuses to repent. First, the believer must be confronted privately. If he refuses to admit that what he has done is wrong, then we are to go to him again, but this time take two others with us. Finally, if that person continues to deny that what he has done needs to be forgiven, then he should be brought before the church. This is an extreme measure and is only used in situations where the person remains very stubborn in his or her attitude. God's Word does tell us that if there is no repentance, then that person is to be set outside the church community until there is repentance. If repentance was not necessary before forgiveness could be granted, then the discipline for unrepentant sin would not be so severe, and the sinned-against would be instructed to "just forgive anyway."

What then should the sinned-against do when their offenders are dead, unknown, unwilling to repent, or unsafe to confront?

For those irreconcilable wrongs done with no chance of repentance from the offender, I suggest a "Revoking Revenge" prayer and counseling model that will help the sinned-against understand that they are owed a debt because of the wrongs committed against them, and will provide a means to release that debt.

When someone sins against another, a debt is incurred. The offender is indebted to the offended. That is one of the reasons God commands the sinner: "Go; first be reconciled to your brother or sister, and then come" (Matthew 5:24). Only the sinned-against can release the sinner's debt horizontally. God values the debt and loss of the sinned-against, so much so that He will not clear the debt vertically unless the sinner repents first horizontally. Still, the sinned-against cannot horizontally forgive an unrepentant offender. For these irreconcilable wrongs, there are three phases for the sinned-against: 1) to remember and mourn their pain and losses with others; 2) to hold the offender responsible for the sin(s) committed against them; and 3) to transfer the debts out of their internal courts to the heavenly court by relinquishing their rights to the debt over to God, who will ultimately bring justice on their behalf. God says: "Vengeance is mine" (Romans 12:19), and He will: "by no means clear the guilty" (Exodus 34:7, KJV).

Just as my student, you'll process what you are reading through your current understanding. I would encourage you to ride out the points in each chapter to the end. You will be tempted to put your past personal and interpersonal experiences into this new framework and judge your previous actions by the new information. Please try to avoid that. You also may realize that the Holy Spirit is prompting you to do something about a particular situation. I would encourage you to be open to His leading.

two

The Pitfalls of Religious Individualism

The student mentioned in the first chapter rediscovered forgiveness in a way that gave him a new understanding of Scripture. When our eyes are opened to something we may not have seen—or you saw it, but you didn't quite see everything the first time, you rediscover its truth afresh. It changes your perspective. My student's world of knowledge regarding forgiveness opened up before him. He no longer viewed Scripture from a unilateral or religious individualist's perspective, but rather from a two-dimensional perspective. This truth not only tilted his world or shifted his understanding regarding repentance and forgiveness, it brought this same horizon tilt or rediscovery to others.

Religious individualism is a unilateral expression of faith that believes in a one-way or one-sided approach to forgiveness. Often, we will interpret Scripture regarding forgiveness, repentance, and reconciliation from this religious individualist's worldview. We will quote those Scripture verses that teach: "Forgive . . . anything against anyone" (Mark 11:25), or "If we confess our sins, he is faithful and just to forgive" (1 John 1:9, KJV).

These verses would fit well within religious individualism because they appear to teach a unilateral or one-way approach to forgiveness that says, "It is just between me and God. There is no need for me to go to you and ask for forgiveness. I can just ask God to forgive me and that should be enough. If you have sinned against me, there's no need to confront you, either. I will just ask God to forgive you, and that should be enough too. Being reconciled to you is nice, but not necessary. Everything is okay between us because I have forgiven you. And if I still feel a wall is up between us when we are together, then I must continue to forgive you."

What contributes to our unilateral understanding of forgiveness and repentance? First, it is natural for our worldviews to become a lens through which we interpret Scripture and understand theology. A worldview is just that—the way we see and interpret our world through our own personal and cultural lenses. Usually, it is shaped by where and when we live, our experiences, teachings, upbringing, religious experiences, etc.

When we read the Word, we are aware that a wide chasm exists between our worldview and the biblical worldview. Different cultures and practices, different historical time periods, different languages, and different authors and audiences contribute to the chasm that exists between the original text and us. Our challenge is to step into the world of the Bible and understand it from within its context before we can apply it to ours.

The biblical worldview and two-thirds of the contemporary world are socio-centric in identity.[1] It is in communally based living that people find their true human existence in solidarity with others. Relationships give life and foster a place to belong. Self-denial and self-sacrifice are characteristic of those in community.

The biblical worldview reflects this *individual-in-community image*—specifically a covenantal community—whereas the Western worldview is more individualistic, with little ties or sense of responsibility to community. From a Western worldview, it is far easier to read Scripture and practice faith from a unilateral, *just-between-me-and-God-alone perspective*; rather than to think about how faith is expressed or lived out in interpersonal relationships with other believers, families, communities, workplaces, or those in need of mercy because of such an individualistic mindset.

WESTERN INDIVIDUALISM

An individualistic worldview tends to subjectively view life through the lens of self-benefit and self-fulfillment. In Habits of the Heart, Robert Bellah discusses how the American struggle for individual freedom has evolved into individualism. Bellah believes the core of what it means to be an American is individualism—the inherent belief in the dignity of the individual, whose rights take priority over the community and society.[2] Julie Gorman, in Community That Is Christian, labels this individualism as "meism,"[3] and also believes it causes us to look at relationships from a self-benefit approach, rather than one that addresses the needs of others. Many Americans seem to believe they are responsible only to themselves. Freedom, to many Americans, means the individual has the right to choose to do whatever is right in his/her own eyes apart from moral absolutes or values.

Doing good is replaced with feeling good

These individualistic desires are rooted deeply in the soil of American hearts and minds. They have penetrated every social dimension of life in which our needs to feel good and to be happy are elevated above our relational commitment to one another—especially in our marriages, families, friendships, communities, church, and working relationships. In in *Helping People Forgive,* Dr. David Augsburger writes that the Western world is a therapeutic society in which "therapeutic values are becoming cultural values."[4] In this type of culture, he believes that objectified moral goodness turns into subjective goodness. In other words, doing what is right concerning another person can become little more than a reason to feel good, and this feeling becomes the plumb line for decisions in life and relationships.

Sadly, this is so true in our society today. Spouses become disposable, families can easily be broken apart, and friendships are discarded for no other reason than one's desire to be happy and fulfilled. Likewise, there is an unwritten sense that no one can judge the actions of another person, because one should not impose one's morality on others. The greater good is established in the belief that a person is being "therapeutically authentic" in his or her relationships. A person acts on the basis of individual needs, feelings, and desires. Furthermore, individualism teaches that a person's identity is not in his relationships, but in his success, performance, and sense of well-being.

According to Julie Gorman, this "me-ism" has created a relationship famine in America. The fallacy of individualism is that it emphasizes only one side of our humanity. It denies our need for each other. It assumes that we are self-sufficient, and we forge our own identities without anyone else. Consequently, it forces us to live in denial of our real need for others. It creates lonely, isolated, disconnected individuals who long for meaningful relationships, but who have no time to invest in them because they are too busy trying to become self-satisfied.

RELIGIOUS INDIVIDUALISM

American individualism has also taken root within our religious communities in the form of religious individualism—affecting how people live in relationship with God and others. It causes people to see their faith as a private and personal matter with little sense of community responsibility. Religious individualists tend to believe they can be in relationship with God without living out their faith in relationship with others or on behalf of others.

Consequently, it affects what they believe Scripture teaches about repentance and forgiveness, and how they live out Scripture in their everyday lives. It also teaches that forgiveness is between them and God alone so that they will no longer have feelings of bitterness or anger, nor experience the emotional problems these create. It is very appealing because many people prefer not to engage in interpersonal relationships or deep relational communities.

"MY faith and MY relationship with God"

Religious individualists view religion as an individual, unilateral experience for which they are accountable only to God and themselves. Faith has increasingly turned inward and become a more personal and private matter—"my faith is MY faith." In other words, how I live out my faith in obedience to Scripture is just between me and Jesus; how I interpret Scripture is equally subjective. Contributing to unilateral faith is the shifting of the confession of sins from a communal practice (James 5:16) to a private confession, "just between me and God."[5] While maintaining a personal relationship with God is key to spiritual growth, religious individualists are less likely to be vulnerable to others, admit their faults, share their personal struggles, or especially ask for help.

Religious individualism keeps the focus on the individual whose faith and practice is more concerned with what my sin does to my relationship with God. There is little interpersonal responsibility taken, especially when it comes to how my sin affects the person I sinned against. A religious individualist is even less likely to think through the results of his actions when it comes to the corporate community or the church. When problems arise, the person who is caught up in the idea of individualism will think more about himself than others. When he sins against others, he is less likely to say the simple but meaningful words, "Please forgive me for hurting you." He is more apt to simply ask God to forgive him without ever attempting reconciliation.

This religious individualistic perspective may even keep a person from getting involved in the lives of others. A young woman shared with our class that when she came into relationship with Jesus, she struggled with drug addiction. So she asked several people to hold her accountable and walk alongside her so she could overcome the life-dominating sin. However, she was greatly disappointed because she could not find anyone who wanted to get involved in her life. They all had their reasons. Some didn't have the time. Others were afraid because they didn't know what was expected or didn't know how to be a support. She had to face the challenge of overcoming this sin alone. She knew the Holy Spirit would be there, but she needed a friend whom she could call and hang out with when the temptation was too great. She did it—but it was very difficult.

Lastly, religious individualists often see churches through the eyes of a consumer. "Did worship move me today?" "Did the pastor make me feel good today?" Church relationships are not seen as something someone invests in as part of a covenantal community, but rather what they can do "to enhance my life." If there are any difficulties or disputes, religious individualists will just go to another church, rather than stay and work it out.

Through the lens of religious individualism, it is only natural that we practice repentance and forgiveness through that same filter: one-sided, for my self-benefit.

"Forgiveness is just between God and me"

Though they had worked together for years, something happened between Jill and Anne that tore their relationship apart. After several months, one of the young women, Jill, sensed God tugging at her heart to go to Anne and find out what had happened. It was obvious that something had taken place, but what? Finally, Jill gained enough courage to call her friend. At first, there was a coolness in Anne's voice that felt more like an icy rebuke, but Jill persisted and went on to explain how much she had been thinking about her. To Jill's surprise, the conversation began to warm, and Anne admitted that she, too, had been thinking of Jill.

After a several minutes of general conversation, Jill got up the nerve to ask what she had done to cause such a rift in their relationship. After all, they had been friends for years, and she did not want anything to come between them. Anne's answer sounded glib, "Oh, I don't know. I've forgotten about it. I prayed about it, and it is gone. I don't even remember what happened."

Jill knew that her friend was not going to acknowledge what had happened. Maybe Anne had "settled it" with God, but Jill's heart was still breaking over the months of silence without even an e-mail saying hello.

In this situation, Jill's friend did not want to acknowledge that anything was even wrong. Anne's silence, though, did not support this. In fact, her silence confirmed that something was wrong—that she was offended by something—but was unwilling to bring it up to Jill. Instead, she unilaterally "had forgotten it." Jill, who never knew what she had done, never had a chance to repent. When Jill called to reconcile, Anne acted as if everything was just fine, even though both of them knew otherwise. Now, Jill is caught in a dilemma: Does she believe her friend that, "It was nothing," and, "It's gone," and reestablish their relationship? Will she continually wonder what the "it" was, and have it always hinder their relationship? After all, she could do "it" again. Was there really even an issue at all? Did she really sin against Anne, or was it something taken the wrong way because her friend has a habit of taking things the wrong way (from her previous woundings) and controlling people by her passive aggressive behavior? Was Anne testing Jill to see if she would call?

This situation is not uncommon in our relationships with each other. Many of us have probably been in similar situations in which people have come up to us and said, "I have forgiven you," and we have no clue as to what we did. Other times, we may not want to be vulnerable and let that person know we've been hurt, so we "let it go," or so we think—only to find it's really not gone. It's equally frustrating to be in situations when you want to work things out because you know something is wrong, but the other person continues to deny it or doesn't want to talk about it. Unilateral forgiveness does nothing to transform relationships because reconciliation is not a one-sided transaction, even though we believe we've been taught to "just let it go."

Unilateral forgiveness does nothing to transform relationships because reconciliation is not a one-sided transaction, even though we believe we've been taught to "just let it go."

"Unilateral forgiveness makes me feel better"

Religious individualism also leans more toward the therapeutic benefits of forgiveness—that is, what forgiveness will do for me. It becomes a more internalized process that ignores any issues of culpability, repentance, or restitution. Forgiveness for religious individualists is a private transaction, grounded in self-love, for psychological well-being, rather than the goal of reconciliation and peace within relationships and community. It moves inward and creates a passive intolerance of "judge not," and causes a withdrawal from injuries or betrayals (Dr. Augsburger). Phrases like "forgive and forget" describe the journey in one's heart and mind without having to engage in the transformation of relationships. This is demonstrated in the story above, and to this day, there remains a strain between Jill and Anne. One was willing to engage in a transformation of the relationship, but the other stood firm—refusing to interact in a way that would bring restoration to the friendship.

INDIVIDUAL IN COMMUNITY

The basic idea of an autonomous individual is not biblical. God created us as individuals, but we were created in and for relationship with God and others. It is in relationship that we reflect the image of God—our Triune God who Himself exists in community of the Father, the Son, and the Holy Spirit. God created us as individuals, uniquely different and distinct. Yet, we find our true identity and freedom as individuals-in-community, a covenantal community. Scripture warns against self-centered and self-sufficient individualism, but not against individuality.[6]

As believers, we are called into relationship with God and with one another in our church communities.

The church is a diverse community in which each member is unique. Jesus was concerned with the individual, and He related to people according to their individual needs. The individual is not lost or engulfed by his or her solidarity with the group; rather it is preserved in the midst of the group. The uniqueness and individuality of that person is recognized within the community. The apostle Paul uses the metaphor of the body and its individual parts as necessary to make a whole body (1 Corinthians 12:12-26). Each part is distinctive, yet when working together, function as one.

As believers, we are called into relationship with God and with one another in our church communities. We are bound together, not because we like one another, though this is a good idea, but because we belong to something bigger than ourselves—the kingdom of God. We also are bound by love to Someone greater than ourselves—our loving, relational God. Therefore, we must live as two-dimensional believers, who find our uniqueness and individuality not in isolation, but in a covenantal, *committed-to-one-another-and-to-God* community. And we must be willing to keep clean slates before God and others.

It is easy to understand why American believers tend to understand Scripture unilaterally, and how religious individualism filters one's understanding of biblical repentance and forgiveness. However, if we are willing to no longer live as one-dimensional believers who express our faith only to God, but rather embrace a two-dimensional relational model of discipleship, we will rediscover forgiveness and begin to understand repentance and forgiveness from within the biblical worldview. Our lives and our relationships will change. And when there is no hope or possibility of reconciliation, our releasing the debts owed us to our justice-making God will bring freedom within our hearts.

three

Understanding the Two Dimensions of Relationship

Whenever I teach a baptism class, I am reminded of my own baptism. I was ready for the "old" Leah to identify with Christ in His crucifixion by dying to all I had become—all that I had done—and having my resulting shame washed away. I so desperately wanted to rise up out of the baptism waters alive, new, and clean. I believed that baptism gave me a fresh start, a second chance to do things God's way, instead of my own. I was ready to live for God.

I was a unilateral believer then and understood baptism from a one-dimensional viewpoint: my relationship with God. Through my repentance and baptism, I became a believer and follower of Jesus, and a member of the family of God; but that's all I knew. Baptism was a public proclamation that I repented, gave my life to Christ, and now belonged to Christ and His church. I was never taught, however, that as part of this new family of believers, I had an obligation to live in right relationship with God by living in right relationship with other believers, nonbelievers, and even my enemies.

I believe we were created in the image of our Triune God for relationship—relationship with God and relationship with others. We were not created for individualism, but rather to be an individual in community—an individual in a new covenantal community. Our uniqueness, individuality, and purpose are not found in isolation, but rather as part of a community of faith. As believers, we have been invited into relationship with God through a new covenant and as a result, we are in relationship with one another as part of a covenantal community.

Covenantal community

Judaism had a communal-relational perspective of the biblical world. The Israelites understood that God created the world, entered into a covenantal relationship with Israel, and called them into a covenantal community. In the ancient world, a covenant established relationship. A bilateral covenant (between two people, tribes, nations, etc.) established a tie thicker than a family bloodline. It was an unbreakable obligation between two parties that was sealed with an oath and ratified in blood that made "your family my family, and your enemies my enemies." Death was the penalty for the one who broke the covenant promises.

Our God is a covenant-making, covenant-keeping, covenant-remembering God who has chosen to bring us into relationship and partnership with Him and one another through covenant. God's covenants are not bilateral, but rather unilateral in that they are initiated by His loving kindness and grace. He sets the terms, makes the promises, and is faithful to keep them. "Persons are recipients, not contributors; they are not expected to offer elements to the bond; they are called to accept it as offered, to keep it as demanded, and to receive the results that God, by oath, assures will not be withheld."[7]

In the Old Testament, God made covenants with Noah (Genesis 9) and Abraham [Isaac and Jacob] (Genesis 12:1-3; 15:18; 17:1-8). He also made a covenant with the nation of Israel and told the people: "I will take you as my people, and I will be your God" (Exodus 6:7). Even when Israel was faithless to the covenant promises, God said: "I will never break my covenant with you" (Judges 2:1). This is because God always honors the covenants He makes with His people (Exodus 2:23-24). He disclosed Himself to Moses as YHWH, the God of Abraham, Isaac and Jacob, and rescued Israel from Egyptian captivity. He is forever faithful and committed to each one of us today. In Jeremiah 31:31-34, He promises a new, superior covenant: "I will put my laws in their minds, and I will write them on their hearts. I will be their God and they will be my people" (v. 33, NLT).

God fulfilled this promise through the life of His Son, who offers His unconditional love to each one of us. He initiated our new covenant relationship, guaranteed by Christ (Hebrews 7:22), who is both the Mediator and the one-time-for-all-time sacrifice for sin (Hebrews 10:1-18). It is His blood shed at Calvary that ratifies the new covenant (Matthew 26:26-29). He graciously gives us His indwelling Holy Spirit to bear witness of our vertical relationship with Abba Father (Romans 8:14-17). Our new covenant relationship is superior to the old covenant because of the superiority of Jesus. Therefore, we have better promises: we have forgiveness for sin with no more sacrifice for sin; and the law is now written on our hearts, so that we obey out of love, not out of compulsion (Jeremiah 31:31-34; Hebrews 8:8-13; 10:15-18).

We enter this new covenant through our repentance and baptism (Acts 2:38) and become brothers and sisters in God's family—His people. We get a glimpse of an early community in Acts 2:43-47, in which the new believers are worshipping God and living rightly with others, sharing with those in need, "and having the goodwill of all the people" (Acts 2:47). *Koinonía* paints a picture of persons sharing a common Spirit, Lord, conviction, and mission where individuality finds fulfillment in community, and where persons and relationships are most important.[8]

As the people of God, we are bound in relationship with Him through the presence of the Holy Spirit. He tells us, "I will dwell with you." The indwelling of God's Spirit binds us to the Lord. We belong to Him and to one another as members of this new covenantal community. If the church is the covenant people of God: "a kingdom of priests, God's holy nation" (1 Peter 2:9, NLT), bound by the Spirit of God, making us family, brothers and sisters—then I have an obligation to live in right relationship with others because we have the same heavenly Father, who expects us to love one another as we love Him.

LOVING GOD AND LOVING OUR NEIGHBOR

Jesus was born a Jew from the line of David, and lived His life in full obedience to His heavenly Father and the Torah. His teachings—a fulfillment of the Law and the Prophets (Matthew 5:17)—come from a Jewish understanding of the Torah. As Christian believers, we must understand Jesus' teachings, ministry, and mission from a Judeo-Christian perspective.

Jesus was asked: "Teacher, which commandment in the law is the greatest?" (Matthew 22:36) and: "Which commandment is the first of all?" (Mark 12:28). This was a serious question. In Matthew's Gospel, we get the sense that Jesus responds to an attack by the Pharisees (Matthew 22:34-40). But in Mark's Gospel, the scribe was impressed with Jesus' response to the Pharisees, and truly wanted to know how He would answer (Mark 12:28-34). The Law had 613 commandments. There was always great debate as to which commandments were weightier or heavier, and therefore more important to follow than those that were lighter or of less importance.

Jesus replied to the scribe's question by saying: "The first is, 'Hear, O Israel: the Lord our God, the Lord is one; you shall love the Lord your God with all your heart, and with all your soul, and with all your mind, and with all your strength.' The second is this, 'You shall love your neighbor as yourself'" (Mark 12:29-31). Jesus quoted the Shema, Israel's confession of faith (Deuteronomy 6:4) and the second part of Leviticus 19:18 to answer the question. Jesus teaches these two greatest commands are inseparable. Jesus commended the scribe's understanding that obedience to these two commandments is: "more important than all whole burnt offerings and sacrifices" (Mark 12:33). In other words, this kind of living and loving is the greatest of all, and keeps us in right relationship with God and others.

Essentially, loving God involves every aspect of our being. It is more than "feeling" love that Jesus teaches. It is an active, fully engaged love.

First, we must love (*agapao*) God wholly. Our whole heart must love God. The Hebrew understanding of heart is a comprehensive word that encompasses every dimension of our being. The whole of our soul (*psyche*), life, attitudes, and emotions must love God. The whole of our mind and thoughts must love God. The whole of our strength, actions, behaviors, and personal struggles against our flesh and sin, must love God. Essentially, loving God involves every aspect of our being. It is more than "feeling" love that Jesus teaches. It is an active, fully engaged love.

Second, we must love our neighbor as ourselves. Love becomes the basis for obedience to the law. If we love our neighbor, then we are obeying the law because "love is the [complete] fulfillment of the law" (Romans 13:10, NASB). Loving and living in a right relationship with other covenant community members—as well as living in right relationship with our non-believing family members, our communities, our coworkers, and even our enemies—keeps us in obedience to the law. Paul teaches in Romans 13:8-10 that if one truly lives in love, the commandments will be kept, and we will be doing what the law requires. It would not be necessary to list all the ways we should not sin or how we should live. If we truly loved one another—owed the debt of love—then we would live and love righteously. In other words, love should keep us from sinning against one another. However, as we know, we do sin against one another. When we do, it does not mean that "love just lets it go," but rather, love engages in the process of repenting, forgiving, reconciling, or revoking revenge because love requires that we live in right relationship with God and one another, as men and women of the kingdom of God.

Loving God and loving our neighbor are inseparable. Living as believers of Jesus, we must love two dimensionally and live in right relationship two dimensionally. Because we love God, we cannot help but love our neighbor. When we demonstrate love to our neighbor, we are saying we love God. There is nothing more important than these two relationships: my vertical relationship with God and my interpersonal relationship with others. If we want to know the love of God and experience His peace, these two dimensions of relationship must not be separated or divorced from one another.

Occasionally, from a unilateral viewpoint, loving God becomes a personal, emotional expression, oftentimes devoid of righteous living. In other words, as a pastor, I have heard countless times, ". . . but I love God," and yet people choose sinful lifestyles with no real struggle to overcome their sinful behaviors toward God and others. Living in obedience to "loving your neighbor as yourself" requires a shift of thinking for religious individualists. It involves expressing our love for God through obedience to Him, as well as doing rightly to our neighbors.

In Luke 10:25-37, an expert in the Law asked Jesus a question:

"Teacher . . . what must I do to inherit eternal life?" (v. 25). Jesus replies with a question: "What's written in the law? What do you read there?" (v. 26). The lawyer replied: "You shall love the Lord your God with all your heart, and with all your soul, and with all your strength, and with all your mind; and your neighbor as yourself" (v. 27). The Lord told him: "You have given the right answer; do this, and you will live" (v. 28). However, this answer was not enough, he wanted to justify himself and asked: "Who is my neighbor?" (v. 29). He may have already believed that he did love God and his neighbor—his fellow Israelites—and may have just wanted to hear again that his understanding was correct. After all, he had just given a right answer. However, as we know, we can never justify ourselves before God on our own merits.

Jesus answers the lawyer's question by telling him the parable of the good Samaritan. The Samaritan, despised by the Jews, was the one who truly demonstrated mercy to his neighbor, unlike the Jewish priest and the Levite. Jesus broadens the lawyer's understanding of neighbor to include anyone in need of mercy and commands him: "Go and do likewise" (v. 37)—just like the Samaritan.

The lawyer's response to Jesus' first question comes from his two-dimensional understanding: to inherit eternal life I must love God and love my neighbor. However, he had a narrow view of neighbor. Loving God finds its fulfillment in loving our neighbors, and this love is demonstrated by loving anyone in need of mercy (e.g., those who are hungry, thirsty, naked, and poor). Once again, we see the link between my relationship with God and action on behalf of others.

"Love your neighbor as yourself"

"Love your neighbor as yourself" does not mean that we must love ourselves before we love others. Biblically, it means that just as we love ourselves by clothing, feeding, and caring for ourselves, we are to love others by clothing, feeding, and caring for them. It does not mean that I must feel good about myself psychologically before I can truly love others. While it is true that if I hate myself I will find it difficult to love others or receive love from others, this passage has nothing to do with feeling good about self. It has everything to do with love being an action word.

Loving our enemy

Not only are we to love our neighbor, Jesus teaches that we must love our enemies as well. In Matthew 5:43-47, He teaches: "You have heard that it was said, 'You shall love your neighbor and hate your enemy.' But I say to you, 'Love your enemies and pray for those who persecute you'" (vv. 43-44). Once again, our relationship with God is expressed in how we relate even to our enemies. This love not only loves those who love us, but also loves those who mistreat or sin against us, or even hate us. However, loving does not equal forgiving. Enemies must still repent to be forgiven interpersonally. I will address this more fully in Chapter 9, *Revoking Revenge and Justice for the Sinned-Against.*

Figure 1 illustrates our vertical and horizontal relationships. It also shows that loving God finds its expression in loving our neighbor. When we do this, we imitate Christ and demonstrate God's love to others. As believers, we cannot live in only one dimension. It is not only about "my relationship with God," it is also about my relationship with others and how we live in a covenanted community. Furthermore, John teaches: "Those who say, 'I love God,' and hate their brothers or sisters, are liars; for those who do not love a brother or sister whom they have seen, cannot love God whom they have not seen. The commandment we have from him is this: those who love God must love their brothers and sisters also" (1 John 4:19-21). These two dimensions are distinct, yet inseparable. That is why Jesus can say the second command is like the first.

Figure 1: Loving God, our Neighbors, and our Enemies

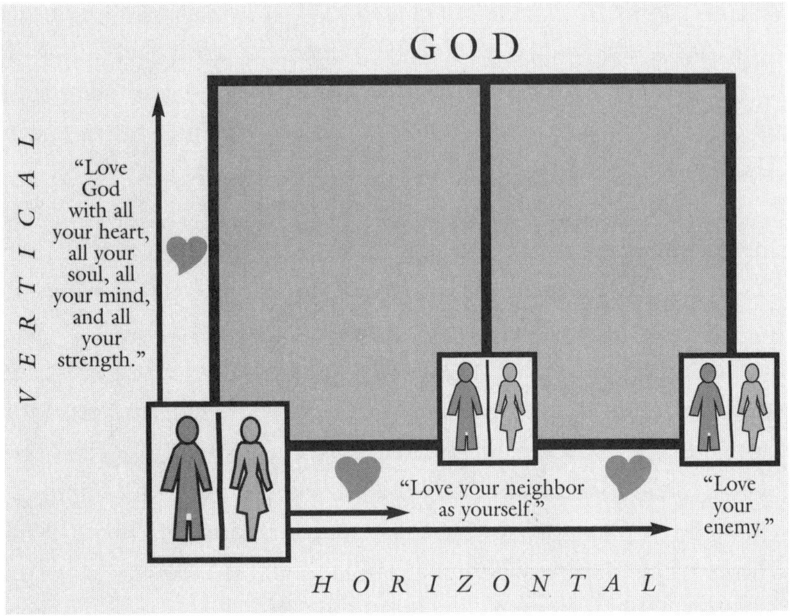

GOD

VERTICAL — "Love God with all your heart, all your soul, all your mind, and all your strength."

"Love your neighbor as yourself."

"Love your enemy."

HORIZONTAL

"The Law and the Prophets Hang on These Two Commandments"

Jesus teaches: "On these two commands [love God and love your neighbor] hang all the law and the prophets" (Matthew 22:40). The Greek word for hang, *kremánnumi*, means to depend upon, "just as a door hangs on its hinges." The door will not function without being attached to its hinges, and neither will the Law and the Prophets be fully understood unless they are attached to love in both dimensions.[9]

When Jesus said that on loving God and loving our neighbor hang the Law and the Prophets, I hear Him saying that if we look at the Law, we will see both vertical and horizontal relational commands. If we read the Prophets, we will hear God's warning to Israel against breaking those vertical and horizontal commandments. These two relational dimensions cannot, and must not, be separated because obedience to the law requires living and loving in both dimensions.

The Law (Torah)

Unlike the foreign nations of Israel's time, who worshipped deaf and dumb idols, Israel's God revealed His name, character, nature, and personal love for them. He made them His people and, because of this, His presence dwelt with them. The Torah, the book of the covenant, told Israel how to live in relationship with YHWH and with each other: "I will . . . be your God, and you shall be my people" (Leviticus 26:12). The Law was given to establish a boundary—a safe boundary—for relationship. God's covenant with Israel established a relationship between Him and His people, and the Law was given to maintain that relationship in both dimensions.

The Ten Commandments (Exodus 20:23-31) and the additional ordinances (Exodus 21-23) reveal these two dimensions very clearly. Figure 2 illustrates the Ten Commandments from a two-dimensional framework. The first four of the Ten Commandments address a person's vertical relationship with God, and the remaining six commandments address a person's horizontal or interpersonal relationships in community.

Figure 2: Ten Commandments' Vertical & Horizontal Relational Laws

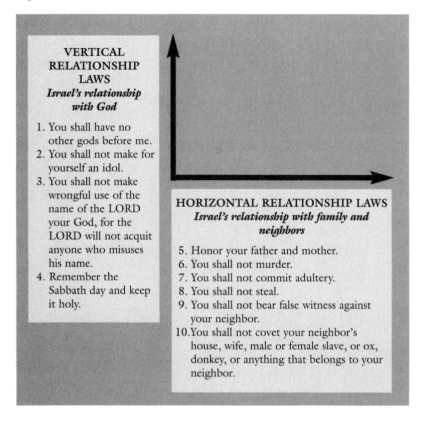

VERTICAL RELATIONSHIP LAWS
Israel's relationship with God

1. You shall have no other gods before me.
2. You shall not make for yourself an idol.
3. You shall not make wrongful use of the name of the LORD your God, for the LORD will not acquit anyone who misuses his name.
4. Remember the Sabbath day and keep it holy.

HORIZONTAL RELATIONSHIP LAWS
Israel's relationship with family and neighbors

5. Honor your father and mother.
6. You shall not murder.
7. You shall not commit adultery.
8. You shall not steal.
9. You shall not bear false witness against your neighbor.
10. You shall not covet your neighbor's house, wife, male or female slave, or ox, donkey, or anything that belongs to your neighbor.

Additional ordinances

"These are the ordinances that you shall set before them" (Exodus 21:1; see Exodus 21:1–23:9) to instruct Israel in the context of two-dimensional living. God's additional ordinances included how to handle both vertical and horizontal situations. Sacrificial laws (Leviticus 1:1–7:22), e.g., burnt offerings, grain offerings, fellowship offerings, sin offerings, and guilt offerings, instructed the worshippers in their relationship with God. Sin and guilt offerings were also made for sins committed against one another requiring restitution.

Horizontal laws concerned the treatment of slaves; cases of personal injury and violence between individuals; the protection of property; how to make restitution for theft; how to handle intentional and unintentional harm to personal property; and social responsibility to the poor, widows, orphans, aliens, and even enemies. The law of retaliation, "eye for eye" (Exodus 21:24), teaches that you cannot take more than what you lost; in other words, it is in proportion to the injury. You cannot take "an eye . . . plus." Justice demands balance. Later, we will address Jesus' teachings on revenge in Chapter 9.

WE SIN AGAINST GOD AND WE SIN AGAINST OTHERS

The Law reveals two types of sins: vertical (we sin against God) and horizontal (we sin against others). If we sin against God alone, we must repent by asking Him to forgive us and then turn the focus of our hearts back to Him so that our relationship with Him is fully restored. However, if we sin against another person, we must be willing to go and seek forgiveness, make restitution with the person *before* going to God to clear our guilt. Sinning against one another is also sinning against God and breaking faith with YHWH (Leviticus 6:2; Numbers 5:6). Jewish piety believes that God cannot or will not forgive a person-to-person sin unless the wrongdoing has first been cleared through repentance, restitution (if any), and forgiveness interpersonally. When that is accomplished, then the offender can go to God and pray that his/her guilt be removed. However, God will not remove the guilt unless there is an attempt at reconciliation.

The Law also reveals that, when we've been sinned against, we must be willing to rebuke that person frankly, not only for the sake of their repentance, but also that we might not incur guilt. Leviticus 19:17 teaches: "You shall reprove your neighbor, or you will incur guilt yourself." The Hebrew word for reprove/rebuke is *yakah*, which means to tell a person where he was at fault, where he sinned. "They were not to cherish hatred in their hearts towards their brother, but to admonish a neighbor, i.e., tell him openly what they had against him, and reprove him for his conduct."[10] Otherwise, the sinned-against may be guilty of sin: not reproving his neighbor or using his neighbor's sin to justify his harboring of hatred against him.[11]

Christ's teaching on forgiveness during the Sermon on the Mount echoes the same priority for the sinner. He teaches us to go first to those we have offended and then return to Him with our offering (Matthew 5:23). In other words, the reconciliation between two people has priority or is the first step (Matthew 5:23-24). Repentance and forgiveness on the horizontal level precede God's acceptance of our gift or God's forgiving us for that sin.

Moreover, sinning against one another is also sinning against God (Leviticus 6:2; Numbers 5:6; Psalm 51:4). All sin committed against one another is also a sin against God and a breaking of covenantal faith with YHWH (Numbers 5:6), deserving of His just discipline and consequences. We can see this understanding in David's confession and prayer of repentance in Psalm 51, in which David acknowledges his sins or transgressions are acts of rebellion (pesha) against God's covenantal law. David's cry: "Against you, you alone, have I sinned" (Psalm 51:4), does not say that David believed he only had to confess his sins to God with no repentance or personal responsibility toward the person he sinned against. David's unconfessed sin was always

Repentance and forgiveness on the horizontal level precede God's acceptance of our gift or God's forgiving us for that sin.

before him—the bloodguilt of Uriah's plotted death, his sin of adultery, and the taking of Uriah's wife, Bathsheba, as his own. David did not confess his sins immediately; it wasn't until Nathan, the prophet, confronted him almost a year later. David could not repent to Uriah because Uriah was dead and he could do nothing. His heart was broken and contrite because he now realized that his sin against Uriah and Bathsheba was also a sin against his covenantal relationship with God. David threw himself on the compassion, mercy, and forgiveness of God to receive his just discipline. God forgave him; however, David and his family still had to live with the consequences of his sins.

Christ's teaching on forgiveness in Luke 17:3 also echoes the same command for the person sinned-against. He must be willing to rebuke those who sinned against him and must forgive those who repent. We'll look at these passages and others later. The point I want us to understand is that Jesus' teachings about forgiveness come from his Jewish background. Furthermore, restitution may be part of the reconciliation process.

Restitution laws

God's laws and ordinances also teach that our actions have consequences. When Israel stepped outside the law by sinning, the way to return to the Lord was clear: through repentance and sacrifice. When they sinned against one another, the law provided justice, which may have included restitution for the one sinned against and a way for the sinner to repent and return to relationship with both God and the one sinned against. The goal was peace in both relational dimensions, and I believe this is what God wants for us today. What was at stake was the *shalom* presence of YHWH in their midst and the blessings of relationship with God and each other. In these laws, there is justice on behalf of the sinned-against by giving instructions to the sinner as to how to take responsibility for sins committed against others and how to be reconciled with his or her neighbor, which may involve restitution.

In Leviticus 6:1-5, we learn: "When any of you sin and commit a trespass against the LORD by deceiving a neighbor in a matter of a deposit or a pledge, or by robbery, or if you have defrauded a neighbor, or have found something lost and lied about it—if you swear falsely regarding any of the various things that one may do and sin thereby—when you have sinned and realize your guilt, and would restore what you took by robbery or by fraud or the deposit that was committed to you, or the lost thing that you found, or anything else about which you have sworn falsely, you shall repay the principal amount and shall add one-fifth to it. You shall pay it to its owner when you realize your guilt."

Again, we read that confession of sin involves restitution before the guilt can be removed. In Numbers 5:5-7: "The LORD spoke to Moses, saying: Speak to the Israelites: When a man or woman wrongs another, breaking faith with the LORD, that person incurs guilt and shall confess the sin that has been committed. The person shall make full restitution for the wrong, adding one-fifth to it, and giving it to the one who was wronged."

David also understood the law regarding restitution. In 2 Samuel 12, the Lord sent Nathan, the prophet, to David to expose his sin. Nathan told him the story of a rich man with many herds who stole a poor man's prized, loved, and only ewe; had it killed and served it to his guests. David's response to this sin: "As the LORD lives, the man who has done this deserves to die; he shall restore the lamb fourfold, because he did thing, and because he had no pity" (2 Samuel 12:5-6).

Restitution laws provide the guidelines for making things right between the sinner and the sinned-against. They also involve restoration of the principal amount plus one-fifth—or in other cases, double, four-fold, even five-fold, depending on the sin against the neighbor (Exodus 22:1-4). If a person has committed any of the sins against their neighbor listed in these passages, they have also sinned against the Lord. He or she must bear full responsibility and pay restitution, and then the person can offer the necessary guilt offering to God vertically. In other words, that person should go and be reconciled by accepting full responsibility and paying back what is owed plus one-fifth, and then offer his or her guilt offering.

Again, can you hear this implied in Jesus' teaching in Matthew 5:23-24? "Leave you gift . . . and go . . . be reconciled" (v.24). Would restitution be necessary to facilitate reconciliation between the sinner and sinned-against before the sinner could seek God's forgiveness? Is this just an Old Testament practice? No, I believe it is true in the New Testament teaching as well.

We see an example of restitution in the New Testament story of Zacchaeus, the wealthy, fraudulent tax collector from Jericho (Luke 19:1-10). Jesus' presence in his home brought Zacchaeus to repentance. He told Jesus he would give half of his possessions to the poor and pay back anyone he defrauded four times as much. Jesus commended Zacchaeus for his act of restitution, because it demonstrated his repentance and brought salvation to his house: "Today salvation has come to this house, because he too is a son of Abraham. For the Son of Man came to seek out and to save the lost" (Luke 19:9-10). Zacchaeus must have understood that in order to become an honest tax collector, his repentance must involve restitution to those he defrauded. His heart responded to Jesus. He was willing to go beyond the law (one-fifth) and this pleased Jesus.

Because of Christ, we know the sacrificial system is no longer necessary. However, asking Jesus to forgive our sins is still necessary. Horizontal confession of sins, making restitution (if necessary), and reconciling (and all that entails) with those we have hurt precedes our asking God to forgive sin.

The law is summed up in love. It was meant to motivate us to confess our sin, offer restitution, and, if necessary, receive forgiveness interpersonally as well as vertically in our personal relationship with God. That same love should motivate our desire to forgive repentant people, to negotiate with graciousness in the reconciliation process, and to revoke our right to revenge when reconciliation is not possible or not happening.

Our God is a God of justice, and He desires for His people to live in community peace.

Jesus' teachings regarding the law clearly instruct us in living obediently to the two greatest commandments in our two relational dimensions. Can you hear the Father saying through the law, "I know you will sin against one another and against Me; I will teach you how to live at peace in both dimensions of your relationships"?

The profound character of God is revealed in the nuances of these laws, and they also teach us how to make things right horizontally. Our God is a God of justice, and He desires for His people to live in community peace. He exerts godly pressure on the sinner to take full responsibility for the sin committed against another by requiring horizontal repentance, restitution, and reconciliation before receiving God's forgiveness for that sin. He also exerts that same godly pressure on the sinned-against to forgive repentant people or revoke revenge, or their own requests to be forgiven will be hindered.

Loving and living are united in the law in our relationship with God and others, and they are united in God's message through the prophets, becoming the basis for prophetic warning and the calling for repentance in both dimensions of relationship.

The Prophets

The Old Testament prophets warned Israel against breaking both the vertical and horizontal commandments. Isaiah, Jeremiah, Ezekiel, Hosea, Joel, Micah, and Zephaniah, warned Israel against breaking the covenant vertically by turning away from the living God and worshipping idols. They cried out for Israel's repentance and warned them of impending judgments unless they repented. Amos also presented God's words of justice and mercy as he called Israel to repent. Far too often, their sacrifices to God were not accompanied by godly behavior toward one another (Amos 5:22-24). Righteousness is always lived out through our relationships.

The prophet Isaiah describes true worship as having a humble heart with accompanying deeds of justice and liberation for the oppressed, and compassionate deeds of mercy for the hungry and homeless poor (Isaiah 58–59). God warned Israel through Isaiah that He was not impressed with their religious acts because they were not accompanied by just or godly actions on the horizontal level.

Vertically, as described in Isaiah 58, Israel was fasting and praying and acting: "As if they were a nation that practiced righteousness" (v. 2), but wondered why God did not notice their humbling and fasting (v. 3). God confronts them for their quarreling, strife, gossip, and fighting with wicked fists. God says: "Such fasting as you do today will not make your voice heard on high" (v. 4). True worship and fasting, however, is described: "To loose the bonds of injustice, to undo the thongs of the yoke, to let the oppressed go free . . . to share your bread with the hungry, and bring the homeless poor into your house . . . to cover [the naked], and not to hide yourself from your own kin" (vv. 6-7). God promises that if Israel does this, then He will say, "Here I am" (v. 9). Then Israel will be satisfied and blessed.

This chapter in Isaiah provides insight into the inseparable link between our expressions of faith—such as fasting, worship, requests to be forgiven, cries for help, etc.—and how we live in relationship with others. Israel is coming to God vertically, doing their "religious" thing, but God is not hearing. Their prayers are being hindered. Why? Because of their unjust behavior towards others! God reveals to them how to correct their sinful behavior so their worship and prayers will be heard—giving Him the opportunity to once again act on their behalf. God is always ready to forgive when our repentance is accompanied by changing behaviors.

PRACTICALLY SPEAKING

An associate pastor from Texas said to me, "Dr. Coulter, if you had presented something that would have required us to ponder and wonder if what you are saying is true, then I could think about it for awhile. But it's too clear, too simple, and too true— and now it's demanding a response from me. I can no longer live as a one-dimensional believer!" He got it; he rediscovered the two dimensions of repentance and forgiveness and now he says he's faced with the challenge to live it out!

Loving God finds its expression in loving others; and when we love others, we love God.

Because the church is the covenanted people of God—bound in relationship with God and one another—our faith in Christ and our righteousness are expressed by how we live with others. Are we living in a right relationship with God and others, and are we doing deeds of justice on behalf of those who are easily oppressed? Loving God finds its expression in loving others; and when we love others, we love God. How God receives our worship and our prayers is directly related to how we live in our interpersonal relationships.

If true worship can only come from righteous living in both dimensions, we must ask ourselves, "Are we going through the motions of worship and religious acts without living in right relationships with others and doing deeds of justice on the horizontal level?" If so, what is the price we are paying? Do we believe our prayers are being hindered?

Furthermore, what role should the church be playing in helping believers negotiate reconciliation, and when would it involve restitution? In the days of Moses and the judges, the law was adjudicated and the people of Israel obeyed their leaders' judgments as the final arbitration in interpersonal issues.

Restitution is not a foreign idea in our courts, nor is it a foreign idea in the biblical world. However, it is a foreign idea in our churches. Religious individualism says, "What do you mean? I said I was sorry. That should be enough!" But is it enough? If I steal from a brother or sister, am I required to not only ask for forgiveness, but also to pay back the full amount plus one-fifth? We cannot sin against one another and just say, "Sorry," to God unilaterally. We must make it right horizontally by our actions that demonstrate our repentance and then ask for God's forgiveness.

Today, we have the courts to help arbitrate and bring justice. However, a courtroom is not always the place that God wants believers to settle their differences. We need a community-based model of reconciliation if we believe relational peace is important for community life to be healthy. We need Holy Spirit anointed peacemakers like Moses in our churches today.

My husband, Bill, is a godly peacemaker. He has the ability—and is gifted by the Holy Spirit—to sit down with all parties involved and help them negotiate a peaceful solution. He asks God for wisdom as he interprets Scripture, and then applies it to those specific situations. The parties must recognize and be willing to submit to the final outcome and to one another. Otherwise, the process will break down. I believe that one of the responsibilities of the church is to help people work through their relational issues for the sake of community peace. If two people are at odds within the church, you can almost guarantee that those around them are taking sides.

Furthermore, when people are wounded or sinned against by church leaders, where can these people find justice? With no one to hear their cases, they may become disillusioned and leave the church or remain in the church, hardened and untrusting. On the other hand, what about people who spread false accusations against a leader (1 Timothy 5:19)? How are those situations handled?

Jesus commands us to love God and love each other. The question we need to ask at this point is: does love equal forgiveness? If Jesus asked us today, "What's written in Scripture about forgiveness? What do you read there?" A religious individualist would say, "Love just forgives and forgets." However, would Jesus reply, "You have given the right answer; do this and you will live"? Or must we now see forgiveness from a two-dimensional viewpoint, and understand that repentance and forgiveness may involve my relationship with God *and* my relationship with others; no longer living as religious individualists, but rather, as *believers before God in a covenantal community*. If so, then biblical repentance and forgiveness will become clearer, and the path to forgiveness will be easier to follow for both the sinner and the sinned-against. Moreover, we will not be far from the kingdom because we will have loved and lived justly in our two dimensions of relationship.

four

Forgiving as the Lord Forgives

"'Father, forgive them!' I've tried praying this prayer and I keep on trying to pray it! I do want to be like Jesus and forgive people because they don't know what they are doing—but some of them knew exactly what they were doing! What does God expect me to do?" I have heard this struggle so often from believers who want to be obedient to the Word—to forgive as the Lord forgives—in order to experience the release of their hurts through a unilateral understanding of forgiveness.

The apostle Paul instructs believers: "Be kind to one another, tenderhearted, forgiving one another, as God in Christ has forgiven you" (Ephesians 4:32). He also reminds us to forgive one another: "Just as the Lord has forgiven you, so you also must forgive" (Colossians 3:13). Paul uses the Greek word *charízomai* to make his point. Taken from the root word, *cháris* or *grace*, this word means "to do a favor to, do something agreeable or pleasant to one, to show one's self gracious, benevolent, to forgive in the sense of treating the offending party graciously."

Another way to say it could be, "Would you be so gracious as to forgive one another?" However, is Paul endorsing a unilateral forgiveness? Is he asking the sinned-against to forgive and forget the offense without requiring the sinner's repentance? No, Paul's idea of forgiveness falls at the feet of both parties involved. The phrase: "Just as the Lord [God in Christ] has forgiven you," reflects how God wants us to forgive others. If the Lord's forgiveness is our example, how then has God in Christ forgiven us? Forgiveness, I believe, lies in the heart and nature of our gracious God.

GOD'S UNCONDITIONAL LOVE INITIATED FORGIVENESS

Our God is a forgiving God—He loves to forgive. It is His nature and character to extend forgiveness because of His unconditional love. God is merciful, gracious, and compassionate. He forgives wickedness, rebellion, and sin, and separates us from our sins as far as east is from west—choosing to remember them no more (Exodus 34:6-7; Nehemiah 9:17; Psalm 86:5; 103:3, 12; 140:3-4; Jeremiah 31:34).[12]

God's initiating love provides the path to forgiveness, reconciliation, and fellowship with our Creator. Paul tells us in Romans 5: "God proves his love for us in that while we were still sinners . . . while we were enemies, we were reconciled to God through the death of his Son, much more surely, having been reconciled, will we be saved by his life" (vv. 8, 10). As a result, we have: "peace with God through our Lord Jesus Christ" (v. 1).

God is the one who initiated this peace from His side. Jesus' death and resurrection make reconciliation with God possible because He desired it. In Colossians 2:13 (NIV), Paul reminds us: "When you were dead in your sins and in the uncircumcision of your sinful nature, God made you alive with Christ. He forgave us all our sins."

Through the new covenant, our forgiveness is secure in Christ

(Acts 10:43; Ephesians 1:7; Colossians 1:14; Hebrews 8:10-12; 10:16-17). God promises to forgive all our sins and remember them no more. However, how do we receive this wonderful gift of God's forgiveness and eternal life?

REPENTANCE AND FORGIVENESS LINKED

At Pentecost, the crowd, in response to Peter's sermon, asked the same question: "Brothers, what should we do?" (Acts 2:37). Peter's reply is still the same: "Repent, and be baptized every one of you in the name of Jesus Christ so that your sins may be forgiven" (Acts 2:37-38). Repentance (and baptism) always precedes forgiveness. God has extended His hand of forgiveness to the world. However, we must confess our sin, repent of it, and take His hand in order to receive it. When we do, He responds by extending His forgiveness to us: "If we confess our sins, he who is faithful and just [loyal to His covenant promises] will forgive us our sins and cleanse us from all unrighteousness" (1 John 1:9).

The fact is that our God is a forgiving God, whose lovingkindness is meant to lead us to repentance

Jesus preached the message of the kingdom of God: "The kingdom of God has come near; repent, and believe in the good news" (Mark 1:15; see also Matthew 4:17). His disciples, too, preached the gospel of repentance and forgiveness of sins (Luke 24:47; Act 5:31; 10:43).

Likewise, Paul preached this gospel of repentance (Acts 26:20). God's greatest desire is for each one of us to come to a point of repentance (2 Peter 3:9)—so much so that all of heaven celebrates when a sinner repents (Luke 15:7). Therefore, we can see how repentance and forgiveness are inseparable. The fact is that our God is a forgiving God, whose lovingkindness is meant to lead us to repentance (Romans 2:4). He does not forgive indiscriminately, for He will "by no means clear the guilty" (Exodus 34:7, KJV).

An extended hand of forgiveness finds its completion in repentance. God has extended His hand of reconciliation, but we must *repent* and take hold of His hand in order to receive His gift of an eternal relationship. We also must be committed to living a lifestyle of repentance (Acts 26:20) and confession of our sins to God with the confident assurance that we will receive His forgiveness (1 John 1:9).

REMEMBERING SIN NO MORE

Because of the superiority of our new covenant with God, guaranteed by the Son of God, and sealed by the Holy Spirit, we have forgiveness of sins. All of our sins can be forgiven because of Christ's one-time-for-all-time sacrifice for sin. God promises that He will: "remember their sin no more" (Jeremiah 31:34). *Remembering no more* means just that—God chooses not to hold our past sins against us. Specifically, He will not hold *confessed and repented* sins against us. His forgiveness separates our repented sins: "as far as the east is from the west" (Psalm 103:12), which is a separation so far that east never meets west. This is His personal promise to us—that our confessed sins will no longer be remembered or held against us.

A young woman sat across from me in my office, anxious and nervous, wanting to say something, but uncertain as to how to put what she was feeling into words. Later, she admitted that she was wondering, "What will she think? What will God think?" Confessing sin to a pastor is often very difficult. However, it is up to the pastor to have the capacity and godly compassion to cross into the world of that person. Compassionate solidarity steps into that world because we all sin and have been forgiven greatly by God. I know the struggle of having to confess sin to another and wondering, "What will that person think of me? How can I say this to another person? It's too embarrassing."

Now this young woman was sitting before me—wanting to tell me something. I knew our gracious God had brought her there and was giving her the courage to open her heart to me. I knew the struggle, but I also knew the grace of God—the One who wanted her to experience the same freedom.

Finally, she said, "I have something to confess to God, and I'm afraid He won't forgive me."

I opened to Psalm 103:12 and read: "As far as the east is from the west, so far he removes our transgressions from us." Then I asked, "Do you know the significance of east from west and the reason God did not say north from south?"

"I don't know," she replied.

"Picture a globe in your mind. If God said, north from south, stand on the North Pole. Now travel down the globe. Which direction are you going?

"South."

"Right. Keep going south to the South Pole. Now make the turn and head up. Which direction are you going now?"

"North."

By now I had her attention and continued to press my point, "North and South do meet. Now, stand on the equator and walk west, and continue to walk west until you come all around the globe to where you've started. If you keep going you will keep traveling west, around and around and around and around. When will you go east? To go east you have to stop, turn around, and go east—and continue going east until you are back where you started. You can continue traveling east, around and around and around. East and west will never meet. In other words, our sins will never stand with us; they will always be gone. God separates our confessed sin that far from us, so that they will never be held against us. Now, we can walk west, turn around, and walk back into the shame of those sins and revisit how we felt, what we did. However, God remembers those sins no more."

When she heard this, her eyes welled up with tears, and she repented to God for her sins. As a pastor, I had the gracious privilege of declaring, "Your sins are forgiven!" with all my confidence in Christ and the blessings of forgiveness through our new covenant relationship. She left, feeling free in the knowledge that her sins were forgiven and remembered no more by God. What a wondrous gift of hope God has given us through the act of repentance and forgiveness!

VENGEANCE BELONGS TO GOD

Our God is a justice-making God. He loves justice and defends the cause of the fatherless, the widow, the orphan, the poor, and the alien—a person who feels abandoned and left to live in a foreign land of hopelessness and doubt (Deuteronomy 10:18; Psalm 68:5-6; Psalm 140:12). So much so, that He says He will hear their cries for justice, and His righteous anger will be aroused if they are mistreated. "You shall not abuse any widow or orphan. If you do abuse them, and they cry out to me, I will surely hear their cry; and my wrath will burn, and I will kill you with the sword, and your wives shall become widows and your children orphans" (Exodus 22:22-24).

The Lord commands: "Beloved, never avenge yourselves, but leave room for the wrath of God; for it is written, 'Vengeance is mine, I will repay'" (Romans 12:19). To avenge means "give justice to someone who has been wronged." No longer are we to retaliate "eye for eye" (Exodus 21:24). Rather, we must release our right for justice to God who will ultimately bring justice.

In Matthew 18:5-6 and Luke 17:1-3, Jesus adamantly warned that he would bring His vengeance upon anyone who causes little ones to sin. He says His vengeance would be greater than: "if a great millstone were fastened around your neck and you drowned" (Matthew 18:6). God will judge injustice and bring justice to the sinned-against. Whether that justice comes in this age or in the age to come—He will not forget!

How Then Should We Forgive?

Because we are created in the image of our God, we, too, must be motivated by love and be willing to keep our doors open for reconciliation in our interpersonal relationships. Literally, we must love the idea of forgiveness, since it is a part of God's nature and plan for us. This is why we cannot separate forgiveness and love—these are two of His attributes, which are within our lives through the presence of the Holy Spirit.

The goal for our broken interpersonal relationships is to achieve reconciliation and peace. We must have hearts that are willing to initiate peace from our side.

Furthermore, this type of loving kindness must not only be demonstrated to those who love us, but also to those who hate us and are our enemies. The goal for our broken interpersonal relationships is to achieve reconciliation and peace. We must have hearts that are willing to initiate peace from our side.

We must be willing to go to those we have sinned against and repent. If we have been sinned against, we must be willing to forgive the offenders who come to us and repent. We also need to be willing to go and rebuke offenders for the sake of their repentance and relational peace. Once we have "won the other" and are reconciled, we must choose not to remember the deed or hold that sin against them any longer.

What about the people who never repent? Should we forgive them anyway? The shocking truth is that God does not forgive the guilty unless they repent. What makes an unforgivable sin unforgivable is the fact that there is no repentance. Unless there is repentance on the horizontal level, that sin will remain with the offender. Once repentance happens on this level, the sin can be forgiven horizontally, and the offender can then ask God to forgive. Until then, the person who has been sinned against must stand firm, pray, and keep the door of his or her heart open to a time when, and if, the offender repents. The offender cannot receive forgiveness from God for that sin until he or she repents to the offended and receives forgiveness horizontally.

How then does the sinned-against find release and peace for his or her heart? By revoking his right to retaliation or justice, and by giving his debt to our justice-making God, the sinned-against can find release from his pain and suffering. Contrary to much of the popular teaching on this subject, true release does not come through forgiving an unrepentant offender horizontally. It comes when we make a conscious choice to turn the offender over to God, who holds the offender accountable for his or her actions. The steps to freedom for the sinned-against are discussed later in this book.

five

Learning to Forgive in Two Dimensions

The young man tried to decide what he was going to do next. From all that he had heard, he sincerely believed that the person who had sinned against him needed to say that he was sorry. However, he was also hearing conflicting messages. Some of his Christian friends cautioned him to let go of the offense and just give his anger and frustration to God. Their counsel continued as they advised him to think of how God had forgiven him and, in fact, had died for his sins on the cross.

As the young man related his story to me, I could sense the emotional burden he was carrying. His question to me was all too familiar. He wanted to know how he could find emotional healing when he felt as though there had been a wrong committed against him and no proper restitution had taken place. Those who support unilateral, one-sided forgiveness say, "Just forgive and forget." However, often the sinned-against respond, "But he never said he was sorry!"

To which the unilateral counselor, friend, or pastor may reply, "Forgive anyway. Forgiveness will help you feel better. Besides, if you fail to forgive those who hurt you, the Lord will not forgive you." Instead of being freed from his or her anger and sorrow, the sinned-against person may feel even more weighed down by a heavy yoke of memory and lack of justice that seem underscored by Scripture. Usually, that person will wonder if anyone cares about the injustice he has suffered, and if anyone will echo his cry for justice.

CHEAP UNILATERAL FORGIVENESS

Forgiveness is central to our Christian faith. However, understanding biblical forgiveness from a unilateral worldview is confusing because we hear two seemingly contradictory voices in Scripture. One says: "Stand praying, forgive" (Mark 11:25), and the other teaches: "Rebuke your offender, and if there is repentance, you must forgive" (Luke 17:3). From a two-dimensional viewpoint, these commands are not contradictory, but rather complimentary, and part of a broader two-step process. For the sinned-against, the first step prepares the heart for the second step of going, rebuking, and forgiving a repentant brother or sister. For the sinner, on the other hand, the first step is: "Go; first be reconciled to your brother or sister, and then come and offer your gift" (Matthew 5:24).

Unilateral forgiveness is cheap. It requires no repentance, no confronting or rebuking—nothing on the part of the sinned-against or the sinner. It just says, "Let it go," so you will feel better. But do those who practice unilateral forgiveness make the sinned-against feel better? What about the one who has sinned against them? That person does not know he has "been forgiven" unilaterally for what he did. Some people have actually said to their offenders, "I forgive you for everything you've done to me." The offender never repented and never changed the sinful behavior. Therefore, forgiveness becomes meaningless to the sinner. We can forgive or release an unrepentant person's debt vertically (to

God), but we cannot forgive an unrepentant person horizontally (or personally). We will talk more about this in Chapter 8.

Furthermore, what I have found is that cheap, unilateral forgiveness creates an illusion that everything is just fine. The sinful behaviors in our marriage, family, friendships, workplace, and church relationships are never addressed. A lack of true repentance and forgiveness creates a façade, and as a result, our relationships become guarded. One of my students said cheap forgiveness is like sprinkling new kitty litter in a well-used litter box. It smells good for a little while, but the odor returns quickly and is dominant again. Cheap forgiveness tries to cover over the wrong without ever confronting the situation or engaging in the struggle to bring the necessary changes into the relationship. Now, if I am the sinner, I may like cheap forgiveness because I do not want anyone to confront me. If I have been sinned-against, I may be stewing because I "keep forgiving," but nothing is changing in my relationship.

Biblical forgiveness, however, is not cheap, unilateral forgiveness. It releases emotional pain, heals wounds, and reconciles individuals. It brings justice to those who have been sinned-against and hears the cries of their hearts. It transforms lives and changes behaviors. It does all these things.

BIBLICAL FORGIVENESS DEFINED

In order to truly understand this concept, we need to take a deeper look into what biblical forgiveness is, and how it is used by God to bring healing and freedom. When one person sins against another, a debt is incurred. The offender is indebted to the offended. A simple way of saying this is: forgiveness cancels the debt. In the Greek, "forgiveness" [*aphiemi*], means *a voluntary release of a person or thing over which one has legal or actual con-*

trol, and carries the idea of "release, sending away, or canceling of a debt that was incurred because of a wrongdoing."[14] It focuses on the guilt of the wrongdoer and not on the wrongdoing itself. The wrongdoing is not undone or wiped out; but rather, the guilt resulting from the wrongdoing is removed.[15]

When we sin against another or offend someone, we incur a moral debt (opheíl_) and that moral debt obligates the offender to the offended. Debt language is used to describe our indebtedness to God, in which sin is equated to debt (Matthew 6:12; 18:23-35). When we sin against each other, debt language is also used to describe the moral debts we owe one another. These debts are cleared when we repent and ask to be forgiven—first from those we have sinned against, and then God. He will not clear the guilty; they must repent to those they have sinned against and then come to God and repent to receive His forgiveness for that sin.

The sinned-against had the power in a biblical worldview

Figure 3: Sinner Indebted to the Sinned-Against

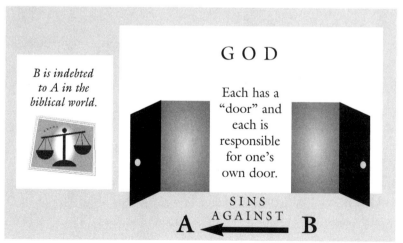

GOD

B is indebted to A in the biblical world.

Each has a "door" and each is responsible for one's own door.

SINS AGAINST

A ← B

From a biblical world perspective, the sinned-against has the power because a debt is owed to them. Figure 3 illustrates this indebtedness. Believer **B** sins against Believer **A** and is indebted to **A**. Only **A** can release **B** from the horizontal debt of his wrong-doing. However, this does not mean that **B** does not have to repent to **A**. We will examine key Scripture passages in the upcoming chapters to help us with the steps and the process of forgiveness. At this point, it is important to understand the concept of biblical forgiveness: the sinned-against one has the power. God desires justice for the sinned-against and reconciliation between **A** and **B** through repentance and forgiveness. What happens next is determined by our worldview, our personal experiences, and our biblical teachings about forgiveness.

If **A** is a Christian who has a one-dimensional or unilateral view of forgiveness and believes that forgiveness must be granted to **B** without **B**'s repentance, then **A** will forgive (or be pressured to forgive) and let it go without ever confronting **B** or asking for **B**'s repentance. Even though **A** has the power and the choice in the biblical worldview, **A** does not feel very empowered. **B** could have the same understanding and only ask for God's forgiveness without ever asking for **A**'s forgiveness.

Both **A** and **B** would be coming from a religious individualist's perspective—one would not confront, and the other would not go and repent, because they do not believe they are required to do so. The misbelief is that just asking God is enough. He will forgive anayway. However, does God only require that we confess our sins against one another just to Him?

Moreover, does God forgive those wrongs that we commit against one another in the place of the offended? In other words, do we really believe that if **B** sins against **A** and goes only to God, but is never reconciled to **A,** that God will—in **A**'s place—forgive **B** without ever asking **B** to clear it up with **A**? We know that Jesus teaches the first step in going to God is going to the one you offended (Matthew 5:23-24). So, we already have a contradiction.

Looking at **A** and **B** from a two-dimensional view of forgiveness, **A** knows that **A** has the power and the choice because **A** has **B**'s debt. That alone is empowering. God sees the debt owed **A**, and will put godly pressure on **B** to go and repent because **B**'s debt cannot be cleared without **B**'s repentance to **A**. What will it take to balance the scales or bring justice to A horizontally? **B** must repent to **A** for what **B** has done.

There are scriptural commands and steps for both **A** and **B** in both dimensions. **A** has options that will prepare **A**'s heart to open the door to reconciliation, when and if **B** repents interpersonally. They will also prepare **A** in case **B** never repents. **B** has options too. He or she can go, repent, and be reconciled; or choose not to go, and have his/her prayers hindered. We will discuss how these options work for both **A** and **B** in the coming chapters, and what happens when the process breaks down.

If my sin is only against God, then it is just between God and me. However, as soon as I sin against another, or have been sinned against by another, it then becomes a two-step, two-dimensional process.

Biblical forgiveness in my relationship with God

The vertical step of forgiveness is a prayer between God and an individual. It initially involves our repentance and entrance into the kingdom of God, and subsequently, our practice of confessing to God the sins that we commit just between God and us. However, confessing the sins we commit against others is only a step that prepares our hearts to go in humility and admit fault, repent, seek forgiveness, and be reconciled to the one we've sinned against. Then we can confess that sin to God. For the sinned-against, it is also a prayer that is willing to: "forgive . . . anything against anyone" (Mark 11:25), which prepares our hearts to confront a brother or sister who has sinned against us, and to forgive a repentant brother or sister. It is a prayer that willingly releases the debts owed us, and revokes revenge of irreconcilable wrongs committed against us by relinquishing those debts to God, and then grieving the pain and loss caused by those debts. The goal of this step is to have a clean slate before God so that no barrier or hindrance exists between my prayers and God's forgiveness for my sins.

Biblical forgiveness in my relationships with others
The horizontal step of forgiveness is a transaction that takes place between people. It involves repenting to those we've offended, forgiving those who come to us and repented, confronting those who do not repent, and disciplining those who are unrepentant in order to encourage them to repent. The goal of this step is also a clean slate before individuals.

Both dimensions are inseparable
We must always keep in mind that our relationship with God cannot be separated from our relationships with others. Matthew 6:14-15 tells us: "If you forgive others their trespasses, your heavenly Father will also forgive you; but if you do not forgive others, neither will your Father forgive your trespasses." In addition, because God already has forgiven us a great debt when we repented and came into the kingdom, we must not refuse to forgive those who owe us a small debt (Matthew 18:21-35). "For the measure you give [of forgiveness] will be the measure you get back [of forgiveness]" (Luke 6:37-38). If I want God's forgiveness for my sins, I must be willing to forgive those who repent to me, or to transfer the debts they owe me to God.

Furthermore, Jesus taught that these two dimensions are inseparable by instructing the offender to go first to the one sinned against and be reconciled before offering his or her gift to God.

Moreover, we cannot ignore the sins we commit toward others or the necessity of going and repenting to receive forgiveness interpersonally before going to God to ask Him to forgive that sin. In fact, we must embody forgiveness by pursuing reconciled relationships, or our prayers will be hindered.

In Chapter 6, we will examine what God has to say regarding forgiveness from a two-dimensional worldview. Biblical forgiveness should not only release the offended, but also hold the offender accountable, and transform the community of faith into a powerful witness of God's abiding presence in their midst. Both the sinner and the sinned-against are commanded to go. The sinned-against is to show the offender his fault, and the sinner is to repent to the offended.

I believe both parties are commanded to go and meet in the middle, because God knows how hard it is to work things out interpersonally. If repentance and forgiveness are not exchanged, the prayers of both will be hindered—the prayers of the sinned-against, if he or she refuses to revoke revenge or forgive a repentant person; and the prayers of the sinner, if he or she refuses to repent to the debtor. The goal, however, of winning the other (reconciliation) is the goal of God's heart—so that His children live in community peace, and so that our worship and spiritual expressions will be received as an offering of obedience and praise. Then when we cry out to God, He will say, "Here I am."

six

Biblical Repentance in Two Dimensions

"I've repented! I've broken off the affair! Will she ever trust me again?"

"Yes, if there is true repentance." That's what Bill and I tell couples who come to us for counseling after adultery occurs. When one spouse commits adultery, the marriage vows are broken. For some couples, adultery destroys their marriages. Couples, who have chosen to stay together and work through the consequences of this sin in their marriages, struggle to rebuild trust and love in their relationships.

"What is true repentance?" one husband asked.

"True repentance is turning from your sin and being willing to work at rebuilding the trust and love in the marriage that was broken as a consequence of your sin. It involves confessing your sin to your wife and seeking her forgiveness. Then it involves asking God to forgive you for your sin. It takes time to reestablish the trust and love with your wife."

Normally, the offender will ask, "How long will that take?"

"As long as she needs," we reply, "because true repentance demonstrates a humble and willing heart to step into the world of your wife, understand her pain, and be willing to do what is necessary to help her process what your sin has done in her and in your relationship together."

From a unilateral perspective, the wife is usually pressured to forgive a repentant spouse and "let it go." I believe she must forgive her repentant spouse, but that does not mean "act as if nothing happened." She has to be able to process her pain with him, which is the consequence of his sin, so that the trust and love in their relationship can be rebuilt on solid ground.

I want to take a moment to recap where we are in our journey to forgiveness. We are commanded to love God and to love our neighbor. We also know that we can sin against God, and we can sin against others. Repentance and forgiveness, therefore, must also operate in both dimensions if we are to live in obedience to these commands.

BIBLICAL REPENTANCE DEFINED

To repent means to make a U-turn away from sin. When someone sins, he moves away from God. Repentance—shuv and teshuvah in the Hebrew—means to return to the Lord. Metanoé_ in the Greek means "to change one's mind and go in a different direction." In other words, to make a U-turn. Repentance is both a decision and a process. It involves a decision to make that U-turn, and then the willingness to engage in the struggle of change by demonstrating the fruit of repentance through the empowering presence of the Holy Spirit.

REPENTANCE IN TWO DIMENSIONS

As two-dimensional believers, sin is a factor that moves us away from relationship with God and with others. When we sin against

God, we are moving away from our relationship with Him. If we continue to sin without confession or repentance, we move further and further away from the Lord. It creates a distance or barrier between Him and us. An unrepentant Christian is an oxymoron. God, on the other hand, is unmoved in His relationship to us. Instead, He convicts us of sin so we can repent and receive His forgiveness. When we repent, confess our sin, and agree with God that what we are doing is sin, we make a spiritual U-turn and return to the Lord.

Remember, when we sin against others, we also sin against God.

If we sin against someone else, we are also moving away from him or her in relationship. We move from a face-to-face position, to one in which we are walking away from or turning our back on the relationship. Repentance on the horizontal or interpersonal dimension involves our repenting to the one we sinned against; thereby, making a relational U-turn to face them again. Our relationships are often torn apart by sin. However, repentance and forgiveness can reconcile our estranged relationships on the horizontal dimension.

Remember, when we sin against others, we also sin against God. We must first repent and be reconciled on the horizontal dimension before repenting vertically and receiving God's forgiveness.

REPENTANCE IS A PROCESS

Sometimes, repentance can be "an about-face." In other words, there are some sins we are able to repent from and never do again. However, other sins are life dominating and require a two-steps-forward-one-step-back repentance. This makes room for the process of repentance. You know when repentance is complete because when presented with an opportunity to sin in that area again, you choose not to do it. When tempted, you stop and say no to the temptation. Then you know God has accomplished His work of repentance deep into your heart, and the fruit of your obedience to Him is evident.

For years, my husband Bill and I were addicted to drugs. In our early walk with the Lord, we began to realize the need to repent of our drug addiction. Each of us had sinned in our vertical relationship with God. Our repentance was a process of two-steps-forward-one-step-back. Each time we sinned, we asked God to forgive us and made a sincere effort to try again. There were times when we would choose not to do drugs, and then there were times when we chose to join in. However, deep within our hearts was a desire to say no, repent, and never do it again. Now that we've been drug-free for almost 30 years, we can say the fruit of repentance has been demonstrated in our lives! Praise God!

CHEAP REPENTANCE VS. TRUE REPENTANCE

We must be careful of cheap repentance in both dimensions. A person who has a spiritual perspective of cheap repentance says, "I'm sorry." However, he or she never makes a U-turn in his or her actions. Instead, there is a continual confession of, "I'm sorry . . . I'm sorry . . . I'm sorry" that flows from his or her mouth, but never a change in behavior, attitude, or action. There is no fruit of repentance because when that person is presented with the opportunity to do it again, the offender chooses to sin. Oftentimes, the offended believer is pressed to forgive the "I'm sorry" offender, and then is made to feel guilty when he or she does not grant forgiveness. This guilt results because he or she still has an unbiblical, unilateral understanding of forgiveness.

If we understand repentance from a biblical worldview, we

would know that repentance demonstrates the fruit of change (Acts 26:20). There is plenty of grace for the process of change because there is "no condemnation" (Romans 8:1) in our struggle against sin. The fact that there is a struggle between our flesh and spirit tells us that God is at work in our lives to transform us into the image of Christ and to empower us to change our attitudes and behaviors. Repentance is really an issue of the heart.

If my heart sincerely desires to change, but I am temporarily caught in a two-steps-forward-one-step-back transformation, then the offended person should view this as my willingness to be transformed and do the right thing—which is to repent and step away from sin. There should also be a marked amount of grace extended to those who sincerely seek to repent and turn away from sin because they are in the process of change, and God is at work in their lives.

> *If repentance is not accompanied by a demonstration of the fruit of repentance in my life, then God is not obligated to forgive me.*

Biblical repentance always brings genuine change. If, however, a person continually professes how sorry he or she is, but never demonstrates a true heart change, that person is not living in a state of true biblical repentance. Instead, he or she may seek to "guilt" the offended party into forgiving him, but never express a true change of heart and action. This is worldly sorrow and regret (metamélomai), which does not lead to repentance (2 Corinthians 7:10).

Being sorry for a sin you have committed is very different than seeking to repent from that sin. If there is no repentance, there can be no forgiveness horizontally. The same holds true for our relationship with God. If repentance is not accompanied by a demonstration of the fruit of repentance in my life, then God is not obligated to forgive me.

THE DIFFERENCE BETWEEN AN APOLOGY AND AN ACCOUNT

Dr. David Augsburger in *Helping People Forgive* discusses the difference between an apology and an account. When asking to be forgiven, the offender can come from two perspectives—either asking to be forgiven by giving an account, or by making an apology. An account comes from the side of the offender and tries to justify, rationalize, and give an explanation as to why things happened the way they did, or why things were said the way they were said. An account appeals to the mind of the sinned-against, and asks the offended to be reasonable and forgiving, with no real acceptance of any responsibility or change of behavior from the offender.

An apology, on the other hand, crosses into the world of the sinned-against and tries to understand the hurt and pain from within his or her world. It offers no excuses and accepts responsibility for the debt owed. It appeals to the soul and heart of the sinned-against by acknowledging the pain caused with genuine remorse. Repentance works best when we are able to step into the world of the one hurt, and we try to understand the debt or emotional damage that was caused by our sinful actions. Remember, the sinned-against one has the debt, and the offender will want to make sure he understands how much he owes and what really makes up his debt. That way, when the offender is repenting, the sinned-against will know that the offender understands the consequences of what he did and will forgive easily. Offering $50 for a $5,000,000 debt will not seem like true repentance to the sinned-against, and the reconciliation process will shut down. We will discuss later how to handle those situations when A is unreasonable and asking B to "pay" too much.

TRUE REPENTANCE MUST BE ACCEPTED

One woman explained to me how she had repented and asked forgiveness for something she had done to a friend. While the friend listened tactfully, she could sense that her words of repentance were falling on deaf ears. The truth is, we must forgive repentant people and give them grace for the process of change. We must also be careful not to require too many proofs or fruits of change.

Sometimes we want to make sure someone is really, truly repentant, so we withhold our forgiveness. We see an example of this very thing in 1 and 2 Corinthians. The apostle Paul confronted the Corinthian church for not rebuking a man who was living in sexual immorality with his father's wife. He then told them to set the man outside the church. In other words, the other believers in the church fellowship needed to steer clear of the man until there was sincere repentance (1 Corinthians 5:1-5).

Later, the man repented of his sin, but the church remained unwilling to receive his repentance and welcome him back into the church community (2 Corinthians 2:5-11). This lack of extended grace led Paul to write to the church expressing his concern: "This punishment by the majority is enough . . . so now instead you should forgive and console him" (2 Corinthians 2:6-7). If we require too many proofs of repentance, it could cause excessive sorrow and hopelessness in the heart of the offender. The goal is always reconciliation between people. Repentant people must be forgiven.

NO CONDEMNATION IN THE STRUGGLE

In Romans 8:1, Paul provides a victorious reminder of God's infinite grace in the life of a believer. He writes: "There is therefore now no condemnation for those who are in Christ Jesus." In Romans 7, he talks about his own personal struggle against his flesh and sin, and encourages the Roman believers to recall God's work in their lives. Even though the struggle between flesh and spirit exists, there is no condemnation from God in that struggle. Instead, the struggle is evidence that the Holy Spirit is alive and well and at work in us. When we struggle to overcome a particular sin issue, the fact that there is a struggle only confirms that the presence of God's Spirit is living within us, and that He is at war with our flesh.

If the Spirit were not at work in us, there would be no struggle because our flesh would be very happy to follow its destructive path without any resistance. In fact, our flesh would not put up any resistance to sin. The resistance to sin comes from the Holy Spirit and our decision to be obedient. As we learn how to cooperate with the Spirit and resist the works of the flesh, we can be encouraged that there is no condemnation in the struggle to overcome sin in our lives. Also, as we repent of a sin that involves the two-steps-forward-one-step-back process, we can be assured that God's love for us remains solidly in place. He created us in love, and He is willing to patiently walk through this process with us until we have reached the point of true repentance and forgiveness.

No condemnation in the struggle also applies to the life of the person who we are walking alongside—someone who has sinned against us, but is trying to change his or her behavior. For example, if a wife is angry and saying sinful things to her spouse, and the Spirit is in process of convicting her of sin and helping her change her behavior, she may have to repent and continually repent until she gets around that corner and repentance has grown into its full fruit. Her husband, seeing that his wife desires to change, receives her repentance and forgives her each and every time without condemnation. His acceptance will help her get around the corner and make a full U-turn.

Repentance must precede forgiveness. Biblical repentance involves not only saying, "Please forgive me for hurting you with my mean and angry words," but also demonstrating the desire to change—with continued humility in changing behavior and in speaking words of encouragement. If we are the one who has been harmed, we must be ready to forgive a repentant brother or sister with graciousness, an open heart, an extended hand, and a willing spirit. After all, Paul reminds us: "Forgive each other; just as the Lord has forgiven you" (Colossians 3:13). We must be tenderhearted to those who come and repent, not requiring so many proofs of repentance that the offender loses any hope of change. However, we must not endorse cheap repentance by either unilaterally forgiving without ever engaging in the struggle to transform the relationship, or by forgiving someone who is not willing to repent and make the U-turn in his behavior.

> *We must be tenderhearted to those who come and repent, not requiring so many proofs of repentance that the offender loses any hope of change.*

Undoubtedly, each one of us will face and continue to face situations that call for us to repent or to forgive. We also need to stop and think about the patience of God in our own lives. He is quick to forgive and restore—and yet, He knows that we will fall short of His plan again at some point in the future. Our desire should be to live righteously before Him, but we can't unless the presence of His Spirit dwells within us. Even then, our fallen nature seeks to drift toward sin against Him and others. However, as Paul reminds us, it is Christ who rescues us from this fallen state (Romans 6:14; 7:24-25). He is the One who empowers us to live victorious lives that turn away from sin and embrace the power of true repentance and forgiveness, so that we can live in right relationship with God and each other.

seven

Forgiveness in Your Relationship with God

"Pastor Leah, I have been taught that I have to forgive the people who have sinned against me on my own—just between me and God—or God won't forgive me. Scripture says that we must 'Forgive . . . anything against anyone' (Mark 11:25), and that sure doesn't leave anything out! I just have to forgive everything and everyone, or I'm in unforgiveness! Doesn't that mean I should just let things go?" This young woman was trying to live in obedience to a unilateral understanding of forgiveness.

"Yes, it sure does seem that way," I replied. "This verse, when read alone or combined with others like it, seems as if we have been commanded to forgive our offenders unilaterally, without ever confronting them. If these were the only Scripture passages regarding forgiveness, then I would have to agree with you. How then, do we obey those verses that command the sinned-against to 'Go and rebuke our brother or sister?'" (Luke 17:3).

"I'm confused," she said. "How do I know what to do?"

The Scripture verses we will examine in this chapter are usually quoted to support a unilateral or one-step approach to forgiveness. "Forgive . . . anything against anyone" (Mark 11:25). "Father, forgive them" (Luke 23:32). "Do not hold this sin against them" (Acts 7:60). And: "Forgive us our debts, as we also have forgiven our debtors" (Matthew 6:12). When reading these passages alone or combined, they make a powerful argument that we must forgive without confronting the offender. However, none of these verses directly address forgiveness between two people. If these were the only passages on forgiveness, then I would believe we have to embody it and teach people blanket forgiveness without the offender's repentance. Because none of these Scripture verses directly address forgiveness between two people, we would also have to forgive without ever engaging in horizontal reconciliation.

How then do we obey those passages that tell us: "Go . . . be reconciled to your brother or sister" (Matthew 5:24)? If we remain unilateral in our theology, then there appears to be a contradiction. "Do I go? Or do I let it go?" However, if we become two-dimensional believers, then these verses fit very well within this theological framework. Again, the verses are not contradictory, but rather complimentary—when understood from a two-dimensional grid. The vertical verses prepare our hearts to extend our hands, and the horizontal passages move our feet to action.

These Scripture verses can also be used as prayers and will prepare our hearts to forgive and extend our hands toward reconciliation. There are no horizontal commands in these Scripture passages. We will explore those in the next chapter.

"FORGIVE ANYTHING AGAINST ANYONE"

Whenever you stand praying, forgive, if you have anything against anyone; so that your Father in heaven may also forgive you your trespasses. — *Mark 11:25*

This passage in Mark 11 concerning forgiveness is set within the context of prayer. However, the stage for this Scripture is set in Mark 11:12-14. Jesus curses the fig tree for not producing fruit, and then enters the temple in Jerusalem and overturns the tables belonging to the moneychangers.

With great authority, He says: "My house shall be called a house of prayer for all the nations" (v. 17). Jesus leaves Jerusalem and once again passes by the fig tree. Peter is quick to notice the effect of the Lord's earlier words. "Rabbi, look! The fig tree that you cursed has withered" (v. 21). Jesus' response to Peter was: "Have faith in God . . . if you say to this mountain, 'Be taken up and thrown into the sea,' and if you do not doubt in your heart, but believe that what you say will come to pass, it will be done for you" (vv. 22-23).

After this, Jesus goes into the context of our Scripture: "Whenever you stand praying, forgive, if you have anything against anyone; so that your Father in heaven may also forgive you your trespasses" (v. 25). The situation of this verse is still prayer. You should note that some ancient authorities add verse 26 to this chapter: "If you do not forgive, neither will your Father who is in heaven forgive your trespasses" (NASB).

Whether your Bible version includes or omits this verse, it does not change the emphasis of Scripture. The connection between forgiving others and God forgiving us is made clear in other passages. You find this same connection at the end of the Lord's Prayer in Matthew 6:14-15: "If you forgive others their trespasses, your heavenly Father will also forgive you; but if you do not forgive others, neither will your Father forgive your trespasses."

Mark 11:25 clearly states: *"Whenever* . . . praying, forgive . . . *anything* against *anyone"* (emphasis added). *Anything* and *anyone* are all-inclusive words. They give a sense of unilateral, blanket forgiveness that covers all offenses of every kind committed against us. A person with a one-dimensional worldview would say we should pray and forgive unconditionally without requiring repentance on the part of the offender. However, is this what Jesus is commanding us to do? His words seem to contradict Luke 17:3, in which we are commanded: "Rebuke the offender, and if there is repentance, you must forgive." Assuredly, we know the Word of God does not contradict itself.

Standing in prayer is a traditional Jewish prayer posture. In Mark 11:25, the "you" is plural, and there is no pronoun used that is specific for *him* or *her*. "When you [plural] stand praying, forgive anything against anyone" (not a specific him or her). It is a general attitude of the heart and a willingness to extend forgiveness to all those who have sinned against us. The context is one of believing prayer. If you pray and believe, it will happen—mountains will be thrown into the sea. What kind of mountains? Could these mountains be "people mountains" or immovable situations that seem impossible? Wrestle through this question with me. Jesus is teaching us: "Have faith in God" (Mark 11:22.)—have faith in the One who empowers you.

This kind of believing prayer (faith in God) can move the immovable (your heart and the heart of the one who has sinned against you). With this prayer attitude, the Holy Spirit reminds you of offenses that happened to you in the past. "**B** hurt me, Lord. **C** sinned against me, God." You must have faith that God will work through your prayers. If you have anything against anyone, you need to have a willing heart to forgive him or her, so there are no hindrances between you and the Father.

The words of Mark 11:25 are a heart-step of preparation for **A**. "Lord, I choose to release what **B** did to me to You. I'm not going to act revengefully against **B**. Instead, I'm going to prepare my heart for forgiveness by releasing my pain and hurt to You in prayer. This way, no root of bitterness will form in my life." When you pray this prayer, you are not pretending everything is right in your relationship with **B**. You acknowledge before God that you are owed a debt, and there has to be a response on the horizontal to actually complete the transaction in your relationship with **B**.

Remember, **A** has the power and is owed the debt. To forgive means to cancel or release a debt that is owed in order to open the door to reconciliation. To forgive, in this prayer context, would mean to unconditionally release the penalty of the offense over to God. It is a release of our right to get even, our anger, and any bitterness that is in our hearts toward those who have sinned against us. When we forgive, we relinquish that debt over to God. However, the offender is still responsible to God for his or her sin. The wrongdoing is not erased and remains with the offender. The offender still has to repent first to the offended and then to God.

Therefore, when we pray and forgive vertically, we release our hurt feelings, pain, and desires for revenge to God. This release cleanses our hearts and gives us freedom in our spirits and minds. When those feelings are released to God in prayer, He prepares and positions us emotionally so that we are able to extend forgiveness to others, just as He extends His hand of reconciliation. The transaction is only complete when we take His hand. This prayer of release prepares our hearts to receive the offender's words of repentance if and when the person accepts responsibility for the deed he or she has done.

When we pray and forgive vertically, we release our hurt feelings, pain, and desires for revenge to God.

Jesus indicates that believing prayer moves mountains. Two friends, who thought they would be friends for life, almost lost that opportunity through harsh words that were spoken in haste and without consideration. Feelings of bitterness began to grow in the heart of the offended woman because her "friend for life" never even acknowledged or admitted that what she did was wrong. The offended woman was angry and afraid to talk to her friend because she believed she would make matters worse, and, after all, she thought her friend should come to her. She became immovable and didn't want to go to her friend who was equally immovable. She did not know what to do about the seriousness of the situation, but also did not want the relationship to be lost. So she poured out her heart to God and asked Him to help work things out. She stood and prayed—and continued to pray and release her sadness, hurt, and anger over the situation to God. She asked Him to ready her heart for whatever He asked her to do to work out the relationship.

In the meantime, God was also at work in the heart of the offender, who began to see the true need for confession, repentance, and reconciliation. Both were now ready—the offender to repent, and the offended to forgive. Neither of these women wanted to give up their friendship. They believed God had something greater in mind for their lives, and they were right. Once the offended in the friendship made up her mind to accept the words of repentance spoken by the offender, a new chapter began in their lives—one that drew their families closer together and brought a tremendous amount of healing to each of them. Believing prayer can move mountains, even if those mountains are in our hearts.

Our willingness to vertically release what is owed to us in preparation for any transaction with another, serves to remove any hindrances in our prayers before God and in our hearts in regard to *winning the other* interpersonally. Taking this step is necessary. However, it is not the only step.

It is what **A** must do as the sinned-against one. God will put godly pressure on both **A** and **B** to do the right thing, but this passage addresses **A** only. **A**'s heart is being prepared through prayer to release the debts. This step also separates **B**'s debt in **A**'s heart from the debts of others who have sinned against **A** and never repented. **B** is not responsible for those debts. No horizontal action steps are given in this passage. Neither **A** nor **B** is commanded to do anything interpersonally here. However, they are both under the same command to be reconciled, which we will discuss later. I believe God wants reconciliation, justice, and peace more than we do. Mark 11:25 opens the door of **A**'s heart to reconciliation when and if **B** repents.

Hindrances to prayer

The Mark 11:25 prayer removes any hindrances between the person praying and God, because there is a direct correlation between the way He answers our prayers for forgiveness and our willingness to extend forgiveness to others. If we are unwilling to release those debts to God, and we are asking God to forgive our sins, our prayers will be hindered (Matthew 6:14-15). If we are unwilling to forgive, release, and transfer our rights to revenge—or even take justice into our own hands—and we ask God to forgive us for our sins against Him and others, I believe God will say, "Not until you release the debts that you are holding to Me."

> *We need to remember that people unintentionally hurt one another, and not every action can be classified as being sinful.*

The apostle Peter understood the inseparable relationship between the horizontal and vertical. Addressing husbands, he said that they were to live with their wives in an understanding way: "so that nothing may hinder your prayers" (1 Peter 3:7). In other words, a husband's sinful behavior—especially when it comes to his wife—can hinder his prayers to God.

One additional point: we need to remember that people unintentionally hurt one another, and not every action can be classified as being sinful. Sometimes, people are socially awkward for numerous reasons—they say and do things that are inappropriate. It may be one of these situations in which God reminds you: "Love covers a multitude of sins" (1 Peter 4:8). Your response might be, "Lord, I know **B**'s heart, and she would never have said that or done that to hurt me. I hold nothing against her." An accompanying release in your heart should follow, and you will be able to relate to that person face-to-face if love, indeed, covered the hurt or anger you felt. It becomes a resolved issue. However, if **B** is an intentional wound-er, and **A** covers, covers, and covers—then something needs to happen in their relationship. Again, it is not about pretending or covering over sin, but rather, it is about being authentic before God and one another.

"FATHER, FORGIVE THEM"

Jesus said, "Father, forgive them; for they do not know what they are doing." — Luke 23:34

"Father, forgive them; for they do not know what they are doing" (Luke 23:34), is the most quoted verse from a unilateral forgiveness viewpoint. The cross is so profound that we will never fully comprehend its theological significance from God's view on this side of heaven. We can only imagine.

The context for this verse also is prayer. "Father, forgive them" fulfills the prophecy of Isaiah 53:12, which says that Jesus: "was numbered with the transgressors; yet he bore the sin of many, and made intercession for the transgressors." Jesus, fulfilling His role as High Priest, is interceding on behalf of those who were sinning against Him. They sinned against Him because they were murdering Him—he was an innocent man, convicted through the testimony of false witnesses, on false charges of blasphemy and sedition. We certainly know that no one really took Jesus' life—He laid it down willingly. However, they betrayed and murdered Him (Acts 7:52). Jesus' intercession from the cross did not extend universal forgiveness to the world. It extended an open hand to everyone—the Father's open hand to receive all those who repent.

Jesus is in the role of **A**, but who is in the role of **B**? Who is the "them" in this passage? The Jewish religious leaders, Pharisees, Pilate (who washed his hands), the Romans who actually performed the crucifixion, and the Jews who shouted: "Let him be crucified! . . . His blood be on us and on our children!" (Matt. 27:23, 25; see also Luke 23:21). They are all the ones in the role of **B**. Peter—who denied knowing the Savior—is in that group as well, along with the disciples who ran and hid, the rest of the known world at the time—and even we were included in "them." Again, Jesus is praying and not dealing horizontally with anyone.

In Jewish piety, what is the significance of Jesus releasing "them" prior to their repentance? Only the murdered person has the right to forgive the murderer. Therefore, biblically, who has the power and the right to forgive horizontally? It is the one who carries the debt. The murdered person is the only one who can forgive interpersonally. Once **A** has been killed, there is no opportunity for **B** to go to **A** to repent and be forgiven by **A**, because obviously, there is no **A** to go to. If the person being murdered extends forgiveness while he or she is still alive, that person offers a gracious release to the perpetrator who still has to repent.

In His prayer, Jesus releases those who were responsible for His death on the cross. He prayed: "Father, forgive them" (Luke 23:34). Jesus willingly asked that the Father to forgive those who would later come to their senses and realize that they had murdered the Messiah. He wanted to leave salvation's door open for each one of us, who through repentance and faith, would place our trust in Him as our Lord and Savior. As I read through Mark

11:25, I can almost hear the Savior's words of mercy and grace folded in between the lines of this instructional passage.

Some scholars say this prayer bought the Jewish community 40 more years (before the destruction of Jerusalem in AD 70), in which they had the opportunity to repent of their sin. After all, Jesus came as Israel's representative. "He came to what was his own, and his own people did not accept him" (John 1:11), nor did they repent. This prayer from the cross prepares "them" to come to repentance when they realize they had acted in ignorance (Acts 3:17). The resurrected Jesus was with them for 40 days, and then He gave an opportunity for the Holy Spirit to open their eyes to the truth of His message. William Klassen, the author of *The Forgiving Community*,[16] believes this prayer reveals the time and situation when Jesus fulfilled His role as High Priest in order for "them" to come to repentance and receive the forgiveness that God was extending to them through the cross. He opened the door for salvation and made room for their repentance. This is true today. People still have to repent of their sins before they can experience God's forgiveness; and that includes the Jewish community as well.

The thief on the cross acknowledged that Jesus was innocent. He also acknowledged his own sin and repented. Jesus promised that the repentant thief would be with Him that day in paradise. However, the other thief never repented and never experienced God's eternal forgiveness. If universal forgiveness was extended from the cross, the other thief would have been forgiven too.

As we intercede even for our enemies: "Pray for those who persecute you" (Matthew 5:44)—we are not forgiving them horizontally, but rather, making room for them to come to repentance. Klassen says that we can pray that they may experience forgiveness, but we cannot forgive people who do not repent or know they need repentance. *To forgive as the Lord forgives* makes room, opens the door, and extends the hand of forgiveness to those who have sinned against us. However, repentance is necessary in both our relationship with God and others. Making room for repentance is God's act of loving kindness; and we, too, must make room for those who have sinned against us to repent and seek our forgiveness.

"Do not hold this sin against them"

While they were stoning Stephen, he prayed, "Lord Jesus, receive my spirit." Then he knelt down and cried out in a loud voice, "Lord, do not hold this sin against them." When he had said this, he died.
— *Acts 7:59-60*

Prior to his martyrdom, Stephen gave a wonderful, historical speech of God's call of Abraham—along with the covenant He made with Abraham, Isaac, and Jacob. He also recounted how Israel was taken into captivity and suffered in Egypt. He told of Moses' faith in God, and how the Lord rescued Moses in order to provide freedom to His people. Stephen used Israel's idolatry to illustrate his point that the Jews killed the Righteous One—just like their ancestors had killed the prophets.

Stephen tied the Old Testament and the New Testament together—showing how they culminated in Jesus, and he indicted the Jewish leaders. The council became enraged at Stephen. Yet, God's servant who was: "filled with the Holy Spirit . . . gazed into heaven and saw the glory of God and Jesus standing at the right hand of God" (Acts 7:55). The men in his presence took him out to stone him because they falsely said that he had blasphemed. Yet, as they were stoning him, Stephen knelt down and cried out with a loud voice, "Lord, do not hold this sin against them" (Acts 7:60).

Stephen was a Hellenistic Jew who was anointed by the Holy

Spirit and full of grace, and who performed signs and wonders. Because of the jealousy of the Jews, there was a secret plot to discredit him. "They could not withstand the wisdom and the Spirit with which he spoke" (Acts 6:10), so they secretly prompted some men to testify that Stephen had blasphemed.

What was this sin that Stephen asked the Lord Jesus not to hold against them? I believe it was the sin of his murder, because Stephen, too, was an innocent victim. Again, understanding this passage from a Judeo-Christian worldview, we can see that only Stephen had the right to forgive those who sinned against him. The sinners in this passage were the false witnesses, the council that heard the accusations and decided that he had committed blasphemy, the stone-throwers, and Saul—who: "approved of their killing him" (Acts 8:1). Now, if the murdered one is the only one who can forgive a murderer, then Stephen—and Stephen alone—had the right to release his murderers. In this case, Stephen is releasing (forgiving) those who are sinning against him—even before they threw the first stone or before they knew to ask him for it. His willingness to forgive the horizontal debt owed him released God's forgiveness vertically, when and if "they" repented.

Saul had an important role in Stephen's murder because Scripture tells us: "The witnesses laid their coats at the feet of a young man named Saul" (Acts 7:58). He was the one in authority over the stoning of Stephen, giving approval for his murder (Acts 8:1).

Once he came to know Christ as his Savior and Lord, I wonder how the apostle Paul viewed his past actions done in the name of God—especially in light of what he now knew to be true: that Jesus was God's Son and the same Savior that Stephen preached about and was willing to die for. The white space between the verses—or what is not said in the text—leaves room for us to consider Paul's repentance over his approval of Stephen's murder, and how he received God's forgiveness because Stephen forgave those who killed him.

Is Stephen's prayer: "Do not hold this sin against them" (Acts 7:60), asking the Lord to forgive them without their repentance? A unilateral worldview would answer, "Yes." However, a two-dimensional worldview would say, "No." Stephen's act of forgiveness released his murderers horizontally because he knew that he would not be there to say, "I forgive you," when they repented. His willingness to forgive says to God, "When they do repent to You for my murder—my side is finished. I release them." That is the profoundness of Stephen's prayer—his heart extended forgiveness in the midst of his martyrdom. We must also remember that Stephen saw the Lord! Looking up at Christ and seeing Him standing at the right hand of God (Acts 7:56) empowered Stephen, through the Holy Spirit, to release the debt of his murderers. God's forgiveness and grace were evident. However, in order to experience the freedom from sin that only God can offer, Stephen's murderers still had to repent.

Jesus' prayer and Stephen's prayer are unique situations and must not be used to endorse unilateral forgiveness. These prayers can be prayed when we are in the position of being martyred or murdered—they have nothing to do with cheap forgiveness. These are very costly, grace-gifted prayers by the soon-to-be-murdered ones on behalf of their murderers.

"FORGIVE US OUR DEBTS"

"Forgive us our debts, as we also have forgiven our debtors . . . For if you forgive others their trespasses, your heavenly Father will also forgive you; but if you do not forgive others, neither will your Father forgive your trespasses. — Matthew 6:12, 14-15

Forgive us our sins, for we ourselves forgive everyone indebted to us. And do not bring us to the time of trial [or us into temptation; others add but rescue us from the evil one]." — Luke 11:4

In the parallel passages of the Lord's Prayer in Matthew and Luke, Jesus teaches His disciples about prayer and the correlation between asking God to forgive our debts *(opheílema)* in Matthew or sins *(harmartía)* in Luke and our forgiveness of those indebted to us. Matthew's petition suggests a completed sense of forgiveness: "As we also have forgiven our debtors" (Matthew 6:12). It also raises a couple of important points. "As" suggests the sense of "because." It could read, "Forgive us our debts *because* we have forgiven our debtors."

The verb *have forgiven* is in the aorist tense in the Greek, and conveys the sense of having already forgiven others in the past—i.e., our debtors, those who have sinned against us or are indebted to us. In other words, we can ask God to forgive our sins *because* we have already forgiven the sins of others who have come and repented horizontally. Or, we have prayed and expressed the willingness to forgive our repentant offenders whether they come to us and repent or we go to them seeking their repentance (Mk. 11:25). The petition to forgive our sins has a condition attached—we must be willing to forgive others their trespasses (Matthew 6:14-15). The Greek word for *trespass is paraptoma,* which means a deliberate misstep, transgression, or sin. "The trespasses committed by one man against another directly affect man's relation to God and in the final judgment will be the standard by which he is judged. Thus a man must be helped to put any failure right

*We can ask God to forgive our sins **because** we have already forgiven the sins of others who have come and repented horizontally.*

(Galatians 6:1)."[17] When someone sins against us, that person's first step is to come to us and repent. In other words, when someone sins against us, we must not take the position of refusing to forgive repentant others. God commands that we forgive, and He will put the necessary pressure on us to do so by refusing to forgive our sins until we have forgiven others. However, we must also be reminded that just because we forgive, we have not earned the automatic right to be forgiven.[18] That would make our justification and reconciliation to Christ a matter of works rather than of faith and grace. Our vertical forgiveness in our relationship with God is forgiveness in one dimension. Because we have been forgiven vertically, we must forgive interpersonally.

As Marshall indicates, Luke's petition suggests a continual "practice or readiness to forgive." Luke is emphasizing the willingness—and the performance of that willingness—to forgive. Again, the petition has a condition attached—the condition includes our asking God to forgive us. We cannot be dependant solely on His act in forgiving—which is dependent upon His grace alone—because we also have a certain responsibility to fulfill. We must repent to those we've sinned against and to God. The verb in Luke is in the present tense in Greek, which expresses a continual readiness to forgive. There is no longer any stumbling block of unwillingness. You get the same sense in Mark 11:25: "Forgive . . . anything against anyone." Having our hearts in a continual prayer posture makes us ready and willing to forgive and release the debts owed to us by and prepares us for the horizontal dimension of reconciliation.

The chart below illustrates the most quoted Scripture verses regarding unilateral forgiveness. These really are "believing prayers" that instruct us to release to God the debts that others owe to us. They are prayers, but they are only the first step in a two-step process for the sinned-against. They are *not* the only step. No interpersonal action is commanded in these Scripture passages for the person who sinned or the one who is sinned against. Chapter 8 will address reconciliation in our interpersonal relationships, and Chapter 9 will discuss what happens when reconciliation is not happening or possible.

Figure 4: Vertical Step to Prepare Our Hearts

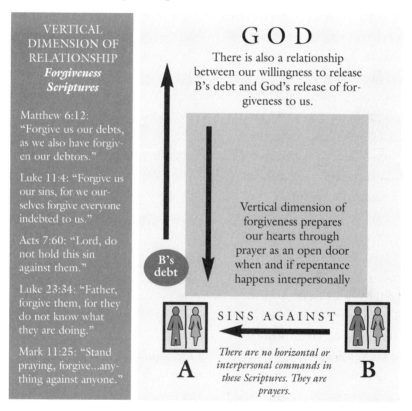

UNFORGIVENESS IN OUR PRAYERS

Unforgiveness in our vertical relationship with God involves our *unwillingness* to release our debtor's debts to God. Instead, many times, we want to make our offenders pay for what they have done. We want revenge. We want them to pay, and we may even seek ways in which others can pay the debt. Also, we may find ourselves being angry with the wrong person, rather than the ones who harmed us; and we "take it out" on others, rather than holding the offender responsible for the sin and hurt. It is not uncommon for people to seek ways to pay the debt themselves in an attempt to balance the scale.

Furthermore, traumatic issues—such as childhood sexual abuse, physical and verbal abuse, and neglect—can create distortions in our relationship with God. Men and women who are struggling to find freedom and release from childhood traumas may be willing, but unable, to release their hurt and pain to God on their own because they are angry and may believe that He really does not care. These distortions keep them from transferring the debts owed them over to God. This is not unforgiveness; it's part of the transformation and healing process. We will explore this in Chapter 9.

FORGIVENESS IN OUR RELATIONSHIP WITH GOD SUMMARIZED

Forgiveness in our vertical relationship is *through prayer between God and the individual.* It initially involves our repenting and entering into the kingdom of God; and subsequently, it involves 1) confessing our sins to God; 2) preparing our hearts to confront a brother or sister who has sinned against us; 3) readying our hearts to forgive a repentant brother or sister; and 4) revoking revenge of *unreconciled* wrongs committed against us by relinquishing the debts owed to us over to God. The goal of this step is a clean slate before God.

Forgiveness in our vertical relationship is through prayer between God and the individual.

Scripture passages discussed in this chapter illustrate forgiveness as the releasing of debts owed us to God through prayer. They do not give us any instructions regarding reconciliation with one another. They are prayers and step one of a two-step process to prepare the sinned-against for reconciliation, if and when it happens. Wendell Miller, in his book *Forgiveness: The Power and the Puzzle,* tells us that this concept, "does not bring reconciliation or make us pretend we have forgiven someone who never repented. It does not make us act as if everything is just fine. It is 'good for the one who has been offended . . . It does not declare the person 'not guilty'; rather, we recognize his or her guilt and give to God our right to pay the person back."

Forgiveness in the vertical dimension of relationship creates a willingness in our hearts to forgive when, and if, the offender repents. It is a way to acknowledge the pain in our hearts before God and invite Him to heal that pain.

If we have been sinned against, when we pray and ask God to forgive the sins we have committed against Him and others, we must:

1. Be willing to forgive/release anything we have against any one to prepare our hearts (Mark 11:25).
2. Forgive those who have come to us and truly repented (Matthew 6:12).
3. Practice a willingness to forgive by keeping our doors of reconciliation open (Luke 11:4).
4. Ask God to forgive our sins.

In the next chapter, we will add the horizontal Scripture passages into our two-dimensional grid, and begin to get a more complete understanding of biblical forgiveness.

eight

Interpersonal Forgiveness for the Sinner and the Sinned Against

Teaching forgiveness from a two-dimensional framework gets most challenging for us on the interpersonal level—the relationship between two people. For a religious individualist, whether we are the sinner or sinned-against, it seems much easier to ask God to forgive our sins against others, and to avoid the confrontation by just forgiving the offender unilaterally. However, nothing happens to change the relationship. Remember the associate pastor from Texas who said, "Now I have to become a two-dimensional believer and am faced with the challenge to live it out!" He *heard* that Scripture commands him to be willing to go and repent to those he has sinned against before going to God. He *heard* that he must be willing to go to those who have sinned against him so that he can bring the sin into the light; and if the offender repents, he can forgive interpersonally. He also heard that forgiveness for the repentant brother or sister should be unlimited. Lastly, he *heard* that unrepentant sin must be disciplined for the sake of repentance. You can hear this young man echo the apostles' cries to Jesus: "Increase our faith!" (Luke 17:5). Jesus' reply to His disciples is the same to us today: "If you had faith the size of a mustard seed, you could say to this mulberry tree, 'Be uprooted and planted in the sea,' and it would obey you" (Luke 17:6).

In this chapter, we will discuss those Scripture verses that move our feet toward reconciliation

You will see that both the sinner and sinned-against are commanded to go and *meet in the middle* to win the other and be reconciled. Remember, in Chapter 7 the sinned-against has been praying Mark 11:25, and has a heart ready to go to rebuke and/or receive the repentant offender. The sinner must be ready to go, too, because Matthew 5:23-24 instructs the sinner to go and be reconciled before offering his or her gift to God. In the *going*, both sinned-against and sinner are under obligation—the sinner to repent and the sinned-against to forgive. Consequently, both will be ready to be reconciled. The vertical step: "Forgive . . . anything against anyone" (Mark 11:25), prepares the heart of the sinned-against to be reconciled with his or her offenders. The horizontal steps move the feet of both sinner and sinned-against toward the reconciliation process and relational peace.

Furthermore, in these Scripture passages, we will see that if the sinner does not repent, the sinned-against is never commanded to "forgive anyway" in the interpersonal encounter. The goal is reconciliation, but interpersonal reconciliation—the winning of the other—can only come through the offender's repentance. It is not one-sided. If the sinner does not repent, Scripture tells us clearly what needs to happen so that he or she will be compelled to come to repentance. If the sinned-against does not forgive a repentant sinner, Scripture once again warns that God's forgiveness for our sins will be hindered. Once again, we can see the inseparable link between our horizontal and vertical relationships.

STEPS TO FORGIVENESS FOR THE SINNER

"Go; first be reconciled . . . then come and offer your gift"
(Matthew 5:24).

"You have heard that it was said to those of ancient times, 'You shall not murder'; and 'whoever murders shall be liable to judgment.' But I say to you that if you are angry with a brother or sister, you will be liable to judgment; and if you insult a brother or sister, you will be liable to the council; and if you say, 'You fool,' you will be liable to the hell of fire. So when you are offering your gift at the altar, if you remember that your brother or sister has something against you, leave your gift there before the altar and go; first be reconciled to your brother or sister, and then come and offer your gift. Come to terms quickly with your accuser while you are on the way to court with him, or your accuser may hand you over to the judge, and the judge to the guard, and you will be thrown into prison. Truly I tell you, you will never get out until you have paid the last penny.
— *Matthew 5:21-26*

The greater context of this passage is the Sermon on the Mount found in Matthew 5–7. In this section, Jesus is teaching from the sixth commandment: "You have heard that it was said to those of ancient times, 'You shall not murder'; and 'whoever murders shall be liable to judgment'" (Matthew 5:21: see also Exodus 20:13). The immediate context begins in Matthew 5:21 where Jesus says that one must not murder; but He extends the murder of the physical body to an issue of the heart when He says: "But I say to you" (Matthew 5:22). One must not even murder a brother or sister with angry words, like raca, which means "empty-headed," or *More,* which means "scoundrel."

In other words, Jesus is saying that you already know that murder brings judgment; but murdering someone with angry words, attacking their head and their heart, equally makes one liable for judgment. It's not just the use of the word *fool* that leads to sin. There is an increasing measure of soul murder implied through the use of angry words. It is literally as if we murder someone with our destructive words. Jesus is pulling it out of the realm of physically murdering someone, and placing it within the inner realm of the heart. You murder another with your anger because the core of that person's identity is destroyed. The explosive anger that Jesus is talking about has some kind of action in it. There's no dead body, but an emotionally dead person.

Jesus then makes it personal by saying that when you are offering your gift—engaged in the process of bringing your sacrifice or worship gift to God—and you suddenly remember that your brother has something rightfully against you (which could include angry words), you must *leave* your gift at the altar and *go be reconciled (diallásso)*. By bringing an end to the hostility, you are then free to come and offer your gift.[20] Some Bible versions insert "angry without cause" in Matthew 5:22—distinguishing between the anger in this passage and righteous anger. Can you become angry "with" a cause? The answer is yes. A person can have a righteous anger that brings about a godly action that facilitates a change. Unrighteous anger, however, usually hurts a person and destroys a human relationship. It is not done for the sake of reconciliation—making things right. Instead, it is done for the sake of destruction and revenge.

> *A person can have a righteous anger that brings about a godly action that facilitates a change. Unrighteous anger, however, usually hurts a person and destroys a human relationship.*

Our interpersonal relationships affect our relationship with God. The idea of *first being reconciled,* and *then coming to make the* offering, instructs believers that interpersonal reconciliation is more important to God than our gifts. Reconciliation removes the wrong or the debt owed. That person can then come back and continue to offer his or her gift *(prosphéro)*, ask to be forgiven, and know that God will forgive.

To drive the point home, Jesus illustrates the importance of reconciliation with a parable. He addresses those who owe debts, and encourages them to settle with their opponents. He also explains why it is important to mend relationships horizontally with accusers. Otherwise, those who have been sinned against—those who are owed the debt—have the right to take the offender to court and get justice and the payment of the debt that is owed. Justice is on the side of the offended, and the importance of balancing the scales, or settling the debt "even to the last penny" (Matthew 5:26), is stressed.

Figure 5: Two-Step Process for the Sinner

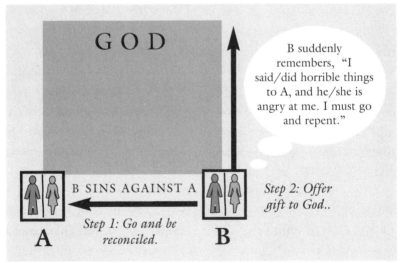

Practically Speaking

Repenting for our sins against others is not just a unilateral, one-step process. Rather, it is a two-step process that is illustrated in Figure 5. If **B** sins against **A**, step one for **B** is to *go* and be reconciled. Step two is *then come,* and offer your gift to God, or ask for God's forgiveness. **A** must forgive a truly repentant **B**, or **A** is in unforgiveness. If **B** is not truly repentant (i.e., says, "I'm sorry," but does not try to change), then **A**, according to Luke 17:3, does not have to forgive or be reconciled until there is authentic repentance on **B**'s part. **B** cannot just unilaterally repent to God without ever going to **A**. **B** can ask God to help him go to **A**, and to prepare **A**'s heart to receive **B**. But **B** cannot just unilaterally ask for God's forgiveness because God will say, "Go to **A**. I will help you find the words and do what is right to be at peace in your relationship with **A**. I am preparing **A**'s heart."

"Woe, if you cause someone to sin!"

At that time the disciples came to Jesus and asked, "Who is the greatest in the kingdom of heaven?" He called a child, whom he put among them, and said, "Truly I tell you, unless you change and become like children, you will never enter the kingdom of heaven. Whoever becomes humble like this child is the greatest in the kingdom of heaven. Whoever welcomes one such child in my name welcomes me. If any of you put a stumbling block before one of these little ones who believe in me, it would be better for you if a great millstone were fastened around your neck and you were drowned in the depth of the sea. Woe to the world because of stumbling blocks! Occasions for stumbling are bound to come, but woe to the one by whom the stumbling block comes! — Matthew 18:1-7

Matthew 18:1-7 (see also Luke 17:1-2) opens with Jesus using a little child as example to His disciples. "Unless you change and become like children, you will never enter the kingdom of heaven" (v. 3). Anyone who is humble like a little child and/or welcomes such a humble person also welcomes Jesus. The world causes people to stumble, but a disciple of Jesus must never cause one of these little ones who believe in Jesus to stumble. Who are these little ones? They could be young believers, who put their trust in those who more mature to lead and guide them in the faith. The warning in this passage is to believers who may cause harm to these young ones—especially in their faith.

Jesus powerfully communicates His stern warning to such believers: "Woe to the one by whom the stumbling block comes! . . . It is better for you to enter life maimed or lame than to have two hands or two feet and to be thrown into the eternal fire" (v. 7-8). It is a very serious warning that could include hell as a final destination for those who fail to believe and obey God.

"Find those who have stumbled out"

Following His stern admonition, Jesus tells the parable of the lost sheep to punctuate His point. The shepherd in this parable is willing to go out after the little lost ones—those who have stumbled out or away because of someone else's sin committed against them, or because of their introduction to that sin at the hands of another believer. The heart of the shepherd is willing to go after the little one who has gone over the hill. The Father does not want any of the little ones to be lost—especially the helpless ones who stumbled.

The "lost" in this parable are often thought of as those in the world in need of salvation. However, the context would say it is the little believing ones who have stumbled, gone astray, and gotten lost. Are they lost because they are the sinners? Maybe. Or could they be lost because they are the little ones who stumbled at the hands of another person—are they the sinned-against? Maybe. Are they the lost, disillusioned ones who once believed in Jesus, but—because of the sin committed against them by another disciple, or because another believer caused them to sin—have wandered or even, in some cases, run away from the sheepfold?

I often see a familiar scenario played out in our churches. A mature Christian in a dating relationship causes a young believer to fall into sexual sin and become disillusioned with Christianity and with Jesus. This leads to his or her wandering away from God and the faith.

Are we aware of this wandering one? Do we have hearts like our Shepherd—hearts that are willing to leave the 99, who are safe, and go after the one who is lost or away from the fold? In frustration or spiritual blindness, we cannot say, "Just let him or her go, because the 99 are better off." Or, "It's better that he or she is gone—no one will find out now." In fact, I wonder how many prodigals *stumbled out* of the church and became lost because other believers sinned against them and never repented? I also wonder what would happen if we—who caused others to sin or stumble—went to look for them, repented, and welcomed them back into the church? I wonder.

Steps to Forgiveness for the Sinned-Against

"If there is repentance, you must forgive" (Luke 17:3).

Jesus said to his disciples, "Occasions for stumbling are bound to come, but woe to anyone by whom they come! It would be better for you if a millstone were hung around your neck and you were thrown into the sea than for you to cause one of these little ones to stumble. Be on your guard! If another disciple sins, you must rebuke the offender, and if there is repentance, you must forgive. And if the same person sins against you seven times a day, and turns back to you seven times and says, 'I repent,' you must forgive."

The apostles said to the Lord, "Increase our faith!" The Lord replied, "If you had faith the size of a mustard seed, you could say to this mulberry tree, 'Be uprooted and planted in the sea,' and it would obey you. Who among you would say to your slave who has just come in from plowing or tending sheep in the field, 'Come here at once and take your place at the table'? Would you not rather say to him, 'Prepare supper for me, put on your apron and serve me while I eat and drink; later you may eat and drink'? Do you thank the slave for doing what was commanded? So you also, when you have done all that you were ordered to do, say, 'We are worthless slaves; we have done only what we ought to have done!'" — *Luke 17:1-10*

In Luke 17, Jesus teaches that it is inevitable that people in this world will cause others to stumble, but: "Woe to anyone by whom they come!" (v. 1). Jesus warns His disciples that if a brother sins, a rebuke is necessary so that the offender will know he has done something wrong and will seek to rectify that wrong by repenting to the offended one. The context is within the church community because Jesus says, "If another disciple sins, you [a disciple too] must rebuke the offender" (v. 3) or confront that believer. Jesus commands the offended believer to confront the offender and to forgive the offender if he or she is repentant. We can conclude that the offender committed the sin mentioned in this passage against the offended—even though it doesn't specifically say, "If a disciple *sins against you.*" We get this idea from verse 4, where Christ says: "If that same person sins against you." Jesus is talking about a personal wrong committed on the horizontal level. The verb to sin, *hamartáno,* can include person-to-God sins and person-to-person sins.

The phrase: "if there is repentance" (v. 3), indicates that forgiveness is conditional upon the repentance of the offender. Jesus tells His disciples there is no limit to this kind of repentance: "If the same person sins against you seven times a day, and turns back to you seven times and says, 'I repent,' you must forgive" (v. 4). The apostles' response sounds like one we would say to the Lord: "Increase our faith!" (v. 5).

However, Jesus tells them they have enough faith. In fact, He goes on to explain, "If you had faith the size of a mustard seed, you could say to this mulberry tree, 'Be uprooted and planted in the sea,' and it would obey you" (v. 6). Once again, faith and believing prayer not only conquer mountains, but also uproot trees and throw them in the sea. Remember, this same believing prayer also prepares the hearts of the sinned-against to rebuke or confront their offender (Mark 11:25).

What did Christ's disciples hear Him say? Certainly, they wondered, "Could Jesus possibly mean we have to forgive and keep forgiving repentant people with no limit? And, could He possibly mean that we must rebuke and keep on rebuking people who sin against us, for the sake of their repentance, with no limit? We do not have enough faith, Jesus, for what You are asking!"

The Lord responds to their cries for more faith with a parable. He asks them: "Who among you would say to your slave who has just come in from plowing or tending sheep in the field, 'Come here at once and take your place at the table'? Would you not rather say to him, 'Prepare supper for me, put on your apron and serve me while I eat and drink; later you may eat and drink'? Do you thank the slave for doing what was commanded? So you also, when you have done all that you were ordered to do, say, 'We are worthless slaves; we have done only what we ought to have done!'" (vv. 7-10). In other words, Jesus is telling them that they are only doing what is required, or commanded, or expected— and *necessary*. When it comes to having enough faith, He makes it clear that they have what they need. However, they must apply it to their lives and to their circumstances. God empowers us for what is required. Therefore, you must believe and have faith in the One who holds the outcome. You do not need an increase in your faith, but rather a faithful obedience to His commands.

Epitimáo means to bring what the person did into the light. "The disciple has the duty to admonish an offender so that he does not remain guilty of sin but has the opportunity to repent; the willingness to forgive, that is inherent in the admonition, is to be limitless."[21] The offender continues to be guilty of sin unless he has an opportunity to repent. That guilt remains because there has been no horizontal repentance and forgiveness. If the offender is unaware of the sin, how can he repent and be cleared? Matthew 5:23-24 instructs the sinner to first go to the sinner and repent before going to God because he cannot clear his guilt until this happens first.

Understanding this from a Judeo-Christian two-dimensional perspective, you can see that horizontal repentance and forgiveness precede the vertical repentance and forgiveness that God gives to both the offended and the offender. The offender cannot be forgiven for his or her sin unless the sin is known, and unless the offender has been rebuked (or made aware of the sin) and given an opportunity to repent. The offended also must be willing to rebuke the offender with an attitude of forgiveness (Mark 11:25), so that the offender can repent and receive forgiveness for his or her sin, and then be reconciled. The offender cannot be cleared of his sin unless there is repentance and forgiveness.

Furthermore, repentance must precede forgiveness in the horizontal dimension. "*If* there is repentance," Jesus teaches, "you *must* forgive" (Luke 17:3, emphasis added). What does repentance look like, and how do you know when someone has repented? The emphasis is upon the repentance. So much so, that if that same person sins against you seven times a day and turns back and says, "I repent," you must forgive.

Repentance is to be measured by a person's actions.

In Chapter 6, we discussed that *metanoéo* means "to have a change of mind *and* behavior." Repentance is to be measured by a person's actions. Cheap forgiveness is granting forgiveness *without* requiring repentance. Cheap repentance is saying, "I'm sorry," but never changing the behavior. If repentance means to make a "U-turn" (or to return to the Lord's will), a person who says, "I'm sorry," and never makes that U-turn has really never repented—according to the biblical understanding. True repentance requires a change of attitude and behavior that reinforces the words, "Please forgive me." If when presented with the opportunity to sin against you in the same way, the offender chooses not to, then he or she has truly repented.

For example, I walk by your foot and stomp on it. I say, "I'm sorry," and you reply, "I forgive you." Then I walk by it again, and stomp on it a second time. I again say, "I'm sorry," and you reply, "I forgive you, but please do not do it again!" I walk by a third time, and I stomp on your foot once more. If I had truly repented and demonstrated the fruit of repentance, I would not have stomped on your foot again after the first time.

However, if I am in the process of overcoming my life-dominating sin of foot-stomping, I will be tempted every time I walk by your foot to stomp it. Should I truly be engaged in the process of transforming my behavior, I will do what is necessary to avoid stomping on your foot. I may ask you to pull it back when I walk by, or to hold me accountable, etc. I may fall back into stomping your foot again, but I will quickly repent. It may even happen a couple more times before repentance has made its mark and I have taken its full fruit into my life.

Remember, there is always grace for the process. It takes time to make that U-turn. If someone is sincerely trying to alter a behavior that is difficult to change, there is grace for two-steps-forward-one-step-back behavioral changes. The offended will realize that the offender is truly trying to make that U-turn and return to the Lord, as well as to mend their relationship. However, cheap repentance and cheap forgiveness do nothing to transform the relationship.

"How many times?"

This is why, I believe, when Peter asks, "Lord, if another member of the church sins against me, how often should I forgive? As many as seven times?" (Matthew 18:21); Jesus replies, "Not seven times in a day, but, I tell you, seventy-seven times" (Matthew 18:22). A true disciple or servant of Jesus must forgive. That disciple is only doing what is expected. There can be no limit on forgiveness because God's forgiveness is unlimited—as long as we repent of our sins. Sometimes, we need grace for the process and must repent several times for the sinful behavior we are trying to change; but our repentance must be authentic, not cheap.

"Go and point out the fault"

"If another member of the church sins against you, go and point out the fault when the two of you are alone. If the member listens to you, you have regained that one. But if you are not listened to, take one or two others along with you, so that every word may be confirmed by the evidence of two or three witnesses. If the member refuses to listen to them, tell it to the church; and if the offender refuses to listen even to the church, let such a one be to you as a Gentile and a tax collector. Truly I tell you, whatever you bind on earth will be bound in heaven, and whatever you loose on earth will be loosed in heaven. Again, truly I tell you, if two of you agree on earth about anything you ask, it will be done for you by my Father in heaven. For where two or three are gathered in my name, I am there among them."
— Matthew 18:15-20

Matthew inserts the passage above between two parables—the parable of the lost sheep and the parable of the unforgiving servant—for, I believe, a definite reason. The heart of the shepherd must be willing to go after the lost. And I believe that the heart of the one doing the confronting in this section of Scripture must go and rebuke the offender with the goal of gaining him or her back. We will see that if the offender does not repent, ultimately he or she must be set outside the covenantal community until there is true repentance.

The parable of the lost sheep tells us that the heart of the one doing the confronting—along with the hearts of the witnesses and the church—must not want this person excommunicated or lost (like a Gentile or tax collector); but rather, that they would repent and be reconciled. The parable of the unforgiving servant tells us that the sinned-against must be willing to forgive a repentant brother or sister because God has mercifully forgiven his own sins.

"If there is no repentance"

No time element is given in the steps of confrontation. Each step may take some time. However, in Matthew 18:15, the sinned-against is commanded: "Go and point out the fault when the two of you are alone." This begins the negotiation process. The sinned-against prepares his or her heart with God (Mark 11:25) and refuses to take revenge on the offender. The sinned-against is ready to bring to light to or expose the sinner's fault—not with the goal of revenge, but with the goal of reconciliation. The sinner, on the other hand, is under the command that instructs him to "leave your gift . . . and go; first be reconciled" (Matthew 5:24).

The godly pressure of not having your sin forgiven unless you come to terms with your accuser, should prepare the offender's heart to listen to the offended with the same goal of reconciliation. If there is no opportunity for winning the other, the sinned-against is not commanded to forgive the unrepentant brother or sister interpersonally, but rather is instructed to take the next step.

Scripture says that if the offender does not listen and there is no chance for reconciliation, then the sinned-against must take one or two others to establish the matter through the witnesses. These people may have witnessed the sinned-against person's issue, or they could be witnesses to the negotiation process. Witnesses should be objective and desire to help both the sinner and the sinned-against hear one another. The sinned-against person may be reacting out of distortions and deeper pain resulting from previous wounds made by others.

The goal of the reconciliation process is to come to an agreement, and then to win the other person over so that healing can take place. The witnesses can help negotiate the issues and try to bring justice. There is an assumption that some of the sinned-against person's issues may involve restitution as part of coming to terms in agreement. Scripture never instructs us to "just forgive anyway." Rather, God's Word indicates that if there is no repentance, there can be no regaining of the other. Repentance must precede forgiveness and reconciliation.

> *The goal of the reconciliation process is to come to an agreement, and then to win the other person over so that healing can take place.*

According to Matthew 18:17, if the second step of the process fails, the issue becomes a covenantal community matter: "Tell it to the church." Remember, God's heart is motivating this process, because it is moving toward a very serious consequence for the sinner. It becomes obvious that there is something happening in the sinner's heart, since he was not willing to repent the first or second time. Now, he is facing a third opportunity. The church now has God's authority to classify this person "as a Gentile or tax collector" (v. 17), as someone who is lost. Is this person still saved? That is up to God; however, I do believe that the path of unrepentant sin can lead a person into apostasy—a falling away in their faith in Christ by their actions. When does this person cross that line? There is no way for us to know. This is strictly for God to decide.

Binding or loosing of sin

At this point, the unrepentant believer is moving further and further away from God, and further and further away from relationship with the one sinned against. In fact, they are so far away, that this person is now outside the community of faith. Unless there is repentance, there is no forgiveness of sin. Jesus then says: "Whatever you bind on earth will be bound in heaven, and whatever you loose on earth will be loosed in heaven" (Matthew 18:18).

The binding and loosing in Matthew 18:18 has to do with the sinner's unrepentant sin. An unrepentant believer is set outside the church community, and his sin is bound to him until there is repentance. If the church is instructed to declare the sinner a heathen and set him outside the community, the church must proclaim, "Your sin is bound to you until you repent." It is agreeing to or announcing something already pronounced by God Himself—unrepentant sin is not forgiven.

We need to remember that the church has been given the authority and the power to declare that sin bound to that person, as well as to loose people from their sins. Jesus, after His resurrection, breathed on His disciples and said: "Receive the Holy Spirit. If you forgive the sins of any, they are forgiven them; if you retain the sins of any, they are retained" (John 20:22-23). He also promises that where two or three are gathered, He will be in their midst. We cannot and must not do anything without the Holy Spirit guiding, directing, and motivating our hearts. Again, the heart of the shepherd must want that lost one to be found, has got to long for that lost one to repent, and should grieve over each step the unrepentant believer takes further away from God and the community.

When people come and confess their sins to Bill or me as their pastors, we can declare, "Your sins are forgiven." That authority comes from God because He has affirmed that repentant sin is forgiven. It is a blessing to be able to pronounce such release. We also must declare the difficult side of binding, "Your sins are held to you or retained until you repent," because it is necessary for the sake of the person's repentance and forgiveness from God.

Do we believe that the sinner can just ask God unilaterally to forgive his or her sin without ever repenting to the one sinned against? Do we believe that God would forgive that sin? From a two-dimensional worldview, the answer is no. The sinner in this passage of Scripture was always under godly pressure to repent and be reconciled. The sinned-against was never commanded to "forgive anyway" interpersonally. The power and debt is on the side of the sinned-against one, and until there is repentance, there can be no forgiveness or reconciliation interpersonally. The sinned-against can take witnesses with him or her, and then tell the issue to the church. Why? Because the sinned-against is owed a debt, and unless there is repentance, there can be no forgiveness interpersonally. The whole community stands on the side of the sinned-against and puts pressure on the unrepentant believer to repent and to be reconciled with the one sinned against. Once the offender repents, the community then welcomes him back.

What does this say to the sinned-against? It says that the debt is valid—what is owed to that person is real—and the sinner must repent before the sinned-against can forgive horizontally. So much so, that there are people in the church community who will stand with the sinned-against and negotiate the process. If that fails, the sinned-against still has recourse. The sinned-against feels valued and heard. In Chapter 9, we will discuss what the sinned-against can do when the sinner has been set outside the community of faith, or is a non-believer who is unwilling or unable to be confronted. These are extreme measures because unrepentant sin must be seen as something very dangerous to one's faith and community life.

Extreme situations require extreme measures

The apostle Paul also understood that extreme measures might sometimes be necessary. Incest was prohibited in the Torah (Leviticus 18:8) and in Roman law. Yet, in 1 Corinthians 5, he confronts the Corinthian church because the members were unwilling to confront a believer who was having sexual relations with his stepmother and was "puffed up" (v. 2, KJV), rather than grieved about his actions.

Paul rightly pronounced judgment on this man from a distance, and bound his sin to him. There was no step one or step two for this man to follow, as Matthew instructs. Instead, extreme measures were necessary for a couple of reasons. First, the sin had to end immediately, and the sinner had to come to terms with his sin. Interestingly, nothing is said about the woman. Perhaps, she was not a believer, because Paul goes on to say that he cannot judge the world, because it is already under God's judgment (vv. 12-13).

Rather, Paul was addressing those who profess faith in Christ, yet still live a worldly lifestyle. He admonishes believers: "I am writing to you not to associate with anyone who bears the name of brother or sister who is sexually immoral or greedy, or is an idolater, reviler, drunkard, or robber. Do not even eat with such a one" (v. 11). Believers who live sinful lifestyles must be held accountable for the sins they've committed against God and one another.

Secondly, it brings the church to a place of responsibility where it no longer just accepts sin—because sin, like leaven, will affect the whole congregation. The church has been empowered to handle such matters.

Paul passes judgment on the sinning believer in the name of the Lord Jesus and exhorts the church: "When you are assembled, and my spirit is present with the power of our Lord Jesus, you are to hand this man over to Satan for the destruction of the flesh, so that his spirit may be saved in the day of the Lord" (vv. 4-5). Church discipline must be done in the name of the Lord Jesus and through the Holy Spirit. In biblical society, this would have had an extreme effect. The intent behind: "[Do] not . . . associate with anyone who bears the name of brother or sister who is sexually immoral or greedy, or is an idolater, reviler, drunkard, or robber. Do not even eat with such a one" (v. 11)—is to not even be in the kind of relationship that would say everything is fine.

This person is in trouble, and the people in the church cannot act as if everything is fine. By remaining silent and passive, you do nothing to help those who are trapped in sin. In fact, you are now at fault. Paul instructs the Corinthian church to do what is right, and to turn the man over to satan so that: "his spirit may be saved in the day of the Lord" (v. 5). In other words, "Turn him over, lift the protective covering of the church, and allow his fleshly desires and sin to have their full effects upon his life, which will ultimately bring him to his end. Maybe then he will come to his senses and repent."

The challenge is the same for today's church. Are we, as individual believers, willing to obey the command of Galatians 6:1-5, and to gently restore a brother or sister who is in sin by coming alongside and offering help? Are we, as the church, willing to engage in the struggle of helping believers who profess faith, yet live sinful lifestyles that are known by all in the church, in order that they may repent and be held accountable to change? Do we believe in the gospel and the power of the Spirit in our midst enough to say with that same shepherd's heart, that those in sin must repent? Are we willing to deliver the tough judgments on sin and the resulting discipline because we believe that unrepentant sin has severe consequences? Or will we be under the same admonition as the Corinthian church for our silence and our unwillingness to get involved and to hold believers accountable?

Repentant people must be forgiven

Church discipline is meant to bring the sinner to repentance. Our heavenly Father loves and disciplines His sons and daughters (Hebrews 12:7-11; Revelations 3:19), and He may use church discipline to do it. In Matthew, the unrepentant believer must repent to the original sinned-against person, receive forgiveness, and then will be welcomed back into the community with a declaration, "Your sins are forgiven." Regarding the sexually immoral believer in 1 Corinthians 5 who was disciplined, Paul tells us in 2 Corinthians 2:6-7: "This punishment by the majority is enough for such a person; so now instead you should forgive and console him, so that he may not be overwhelmed by excessive sorrow."

In other words, the discipline had its effect; it motivated the sinner to repent, and now it was time to forgive him for this sin, comfort him, and welcome him back into the fellowship. Otherwise, satan may use his excessive sorrow to discourage him

We must be careful that we do not require more of a person than God requires—so many fruits of repentance that the offender feels as though he or she will never be able to be good enough to be welcomed back.

and drive him away from faith in Christ. Paul admonishes the Corinthian church to forgive and continues by saying: "Anyone whom you forgive, I also forgive" (2 Corinthians 2:10). Declaring forgiveness brings comfort, healing, and lifts the grieving heart. Again, we see how God has given the church authority to declare sins forgiven or bound. "Whatever you bind [unrepentant sins] . . . will be bound . . . and whatever you loose [forgiveness after repentance] . . . will be loosed" (Matthew 18:18), in agreement and in the presence of Jesus.

Paul warns the Corinthian church again; but this time, he admonishes them to forgive the man because he has repented. If the church requires too many proofs of repentance and is unwilling to forgive, then it becomes an open door for the enemy's attacks of sorrow, discouragement, and feelings of isolation. We must be careful that we do not require more of a person than God requires—so many fruits of repentance that the offender feels as though he or she will never be able to be good enough to be welcomed back.

Returning to Matthew 18, Jesus answers Peter's questions with a parable. Peter has just asked with astonishment: "Lord, if another member of the church sins against me, how often should I forgive? As many as seven times?" (v. 21). Jesus answers: "Not seven times, but I tell you, seventy-seven times" (v. 22). Then the Lord tells them the parable of the unforgiving servant, to explain to Peter and His disciples why forgiveness of repentant others has no limit.

Debt language, repentance, forgiveness, unwillingness to forgive, and its consequences are all illustrated in the story of a king, a slave, a fellow slave, and the community. This parable is often quoted to support a unilateral view of forgiveness. The words, "Because God has forgiven you a big debt, you must forgive others, or He will turn you over to the torturers," are often used to encourage the sinned-against to forgive unrepentant people, but is that the point of the parable?

The king wanted to settle his accounts and called in those who owed him money. The one who owed him 10,000 talents could not pay the debt, and he fell to his knees begging for patience with a promise to repay all that he owed. The king had compassion on the man and released, pardoned, and forgave him. However, given the same opportunity to extend compassion and mercy, this forgiven slave failed to do so. In fact, he finds a man who owes him 100 denarii, seizes him, and threatens him if he does not repay. His fellow slave does exactly the same thing he did in front of the king—begs for patience with a promise to repay what he owed. However, he refuses and throws him into debtor's prison until the entire debt is paid. The community witnesses this injustice and tells the king—who then withdraws his forgiveness of the debt and turns the slave over to debtor's prison until he can pay back what was owed.

"How many times should I forgive my *repentant* brother,

Jesus?"

"Unlimited times—no limit, Peter—always."

Because you have been forgiven so much, when someone comes to you and repents, you must forgive. A unilateral view does not see the repentance on the part of the second slave and says, "Just forgive without ever requiring repentance, or God will turn you over to the torturers." However, a two-dimensional view says, "When someone repents to you and acknowledges that they owe you a debt, you must forgive." The slave was in trouble with the king not because he wanted payment of the debt that was owed him by his fellow slave, but because he attempted to extract payment without extending the same compassion and generous forgiveness to the man that he had received. In other words, believers who ask God to forgive them for their sins must be willing to forgive those who repent to them for sins committed against them. Believers must not withhold forgiveness because we are all indebted to the King of kings.

How many times? No limit, if there is repentance interpersonally.

How do you gain a brother or sister who has sinned against you? You win that brother or sister by going—and you keep going until there is repentance and forgiveness. How many times must I forgive? On the horizontal level, every time there is repentance. In the vertical—every time you pray, you release your right to get even. Our response is much like the disciples: "Lord, increase our faith!" (Luke 17:5). It is much easier just to "let it go" without ever engaging in the process. I can hear Jesus say, "You have what you need—you have My Spirit to instruct you in the process and to empower you to live righteously—not only for your sake, but for the sake of others and relational peace."

Repentance, forgiveness, and consequences

When extreme situations arise, we must be willing to take extreme measures. For example, if a pedophile abuses a child in our church, extreme measures must be taken to remove that person from the congregation. We believe in restoration, but we must be wise. Too many Christians with a unilateral worldview want to believe that everything is just fine as soon as the person has repented. "He is a changed man or she is a different woman now. It's no longer an issue." However, actions must have consequences. We are biblical—not legalistic—because we hold people responsible for their sins. Child abuse is a crime. Holding people responsible to the law and allowing them to face the consequences of their sins and crimes is the biblical thing to do.

As pastors, a woman may come and confess a sin, for example, embezzlement. Our responsibility is to help her repent to God and to her employer, pay back what is owed, and make restitution. What would it say to her employer, the sinned against one, if she repented to him and gave him back the money plus one-fifth? What if her employer was a nonbeliever? What would it say to him then? That Christians are thieves? Maybe, but more than likely, it would say Christians are in process and have problems, too; but they answer to God—and He is concerned about the debt owed the nonbeliever. If we do what is right, who knows what could happen? Her employer may press charges, and she may have to go to court and end up serving time in jail. Or, he may forgive her and extend mercy to her. Regardless of the outcome, we must take responsibility and be willing to walk alongside this person—not only as she goes through the stages of repentance, but also as she faces the consequence of her sin. God can use these consequences in her life to bring about the kind of change necessary for her transformation.

I believe the Holy Spirit is at work in a believer's life, and when He reveals something, or exposes someone's sin, it is to bring healing and restoration. God reveals to heal, but never to condemn us. He wants to set us free from sin, and He knows that sins done in secret keep us bound. As parents, if we always prevent our children from experiencing the consequences of their actions by minimizing or rationalizing what they have done, then we are not fulfilling our responsibility before God. They will grow up and never understand the full weight of sin and the sorrow it brings to themselves and to those they've sinned against.

When we look at life through rose-colored glasses, we miss opportunities for people to be transformed because the weight of the sin has not really hit them. Often, we want to find a way to "make things right," minimize the weight, or take away the consequences. However, if we do this, we risk missing what God wants to do in the lives of others. Loving one another involves a compassionate love that understands the seriousness of sin and its consequences in our own lives and in the lives of others, while seeking to cooperate with Holy Spirit in the lives of the sinner, the sinned-against, and the one called alongside to help.

> *When we look at life through rose-colored glasses, we miss opportunities for people to be transformed because the weight of the sin has not really hit them.*

INTERPERSONAL FORGIVENESS SUMMARIZED

The interpersonal dimension of forgiveness is part of the two-step process. Figure 9 illustrates these two steps in both relational dimensions. For the sinner, step one is to go to the sinned-against, repent, be forgiven, and be reconciled. Step two includes asking for God's forgiveness.

For the sinned-against, step one involves going to God in prayer and releasing the debts owed. It is at this point, that the person grieves out the anger and pain caused by the sinner.

In step two, the person is to go and rebuke the offender. If he or she repents, the person who has been sinned against must forgive and be reconciled. Boundaries may be necessary to re-establish trust in the relationship (see Chapter 10). If there is no repentance, there can be no forgiveness interpersonally. The unrepentant believer's sin remains unforgiven by God until he or she repents to the one sinned against. As Figure 6 illustrates, there can never be a step two for **B** unless **B** repents, and there can never be a step two for **A** until **B** repents. Repentance is necessary for interpersonal forgiveness.

Figure 6: A Two-Step, Two-Dimensional Process for Sinner and Sinned-Against

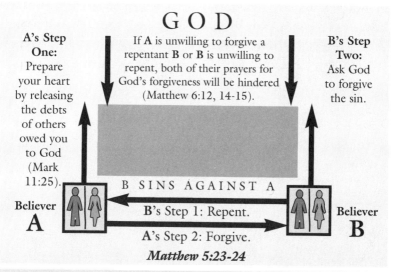

B's only command is to go and be reconciled through repentance to **A**, and then come and ask God to forgive your sin. **A**'s heart is prepared to forgive a repentant **B** through the Mark 11:25 command: "Stand praying, forgive . . . anything against anyone." If **B** repents, **A** forgives **B**; it is a winning of the other. If **B** does not repent, **A** has other options.

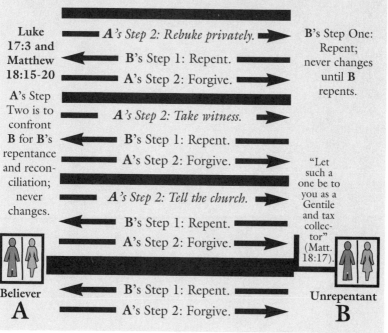

Forgiveness is a willingness of the heart to express pardon that invites repentance. However, unless the offender repents, there can be no reconciliation. The wrongdoing is unforgivable because **B** will not repent. What does believer **A** do when **B** does not repent? The Mark 11:25 command still stands—believing prayer can move mountains!

nine

Revoking Revenge and Justice for the Sinned Against

Irreconcilable wrongs are the most painful to grieve out. For the past 25 years, I've sat with people in the ashes of their lives—those whose worlds have collapsed around them because of others' sins committed against them in their childhoods with no opportunities for repentance or justice. A teary-eyed woman sat with me and began to tell me about her difficulties in her relationship with God, and how hard it was for her to believe in a loving and caring God.

She said, "Worship is too hard and reading the Bible is almost impossible! I'm angry at God and everyone else! Why would He let me be abused when I was a child? Why didn't He care enough to stop the abuse? It's too hard for me, Pastor Leah, to believe that God cares about me now! I can't forgive that person—I won't forgive that person—because it's not fair; it's not just! What about me? Doesn't anyone care about what happened to me? How am I ever going to find freedom from this captivity to my past?"

CRY FOR JUSTICE FROM THE INTERNAL COURT

When we have been sinned against, Mark 11:25 instructs us to release anything we are holding against anyone. This verse prepares our hearts for emotional healing. If the offender is available and known, there is a chance for reconciliation. If the offender agrees to meet with us and is truly repentant, we will be ready to forgive. Even if the offender does not come, we can go to them and bring the issues to light with the goal of reconciliation. Furthermore, if the offender is available but never repents, it enables us to continue to stand praying—extending our hands toward reconciliation when and if that offender repents.

However, some wrongs are irreconcilable. They are irreconcilable not only when the offender is unwilling to repent, but also unable to repent—dead or mentally incapacitated—unknown, unable to be found, or is unsafe to confront. Interpersonal relationships cannot be restored unilaterally. The path to forgiveness for irreconcilable wrongs is to help the sinned-against cry out for justice to our God, who hears and will meet them in the pain of their losses. The vertical step is now a prayer between God and the sinned-against involving the process of grieving over the losses incurred, revoking their rights to balance the scale, and transferring their debts to a God who will hold the offender accountable for his or her sins.

As previously stated, when a sin is committed against another, a debt is incurred and payment is required to clear the debt. Someone has to pay the debt. Justice hinges upon the payment of such a debt (the balancing of the scales). In our vertical relationship with God, we owed a debt to God that had to be paid—and we could not pay it. Jesus paid the sin-debt we owed to God. However, repentance must precede forgiveness before we are reconciled to God and receive His gift of salvation. When we've been sinned against, we are owed a debt from the one who harmed us.

Justice comes to us when that person repents and the debt is cleared between us. If the person is unable or unwilling to repent or is unsafe to confront, the debt cannot be cleared, and our cry for justice goes up to God.

With irreconcilable wrongs, the sinned-against cry out for justice from the internal courtroom of their hearts, presenting evidence upon evidence in an effort to determine the reason for the injustice. They try to find someone who will agree that what happened to them was wrong. The sinned-against take all roles in that internal courtroom. As the prosecuting attorney, they present their evidence for their fault for its occurrence. As the defense attorney, they try to defend the ones who harmed them. As the judge, they look disapprovingly at themselves, waiting for the gavel to come down. As the jury, they declare themselves, "Guilty!" and sentence themselves to a life of captivity.

God hears the cries of the sinned-against for justice, whether silenced by death or muted by others. God heard Abel's blood crying out from the ground (Genesis 4:10), Ishmael's cries in the wilderness (Genesis 21:17), and Israel's cries because of their Egyptian captivity (Exodus 3:7). God always hears the cries of the oppressed and helpless, and He will avenge or bring justice. He does not ignore our tears. He counts each one (Psalm 56:8).

God hears the cries of the sinned-against for justice, whether silenced by death or muted by others.

The Holy Spirit is present with believers and has a view from within their internal world. He is our Paraclete—our Comforter and Advocate who comes alongside us and echoes our cries for justice from within our internal courts. He also intercedes with groans to the Father on our behalf (Romans 8:26-27), because there are times we do not know how to pray. In our weakness and helplessness, the Holy Spirit comes with help and assistance *(synantilambánomai)* through His intercession on our behalf. He pleads for us with unspoken prayers, the groaning *(stenagmós)* and sighing as of the oppressed. Understanding the inarticulate pain of the sinned-against and their cries for justice, the Holy Spirit intercedes for their rescue and liberation.

The path to forgiveness for irreconcilable wrongs does not encourage the sinned-against to "forgive and forget" an unrepentant offender, but to transfer the debts owed them to our avenging God.

"NEVER AVENGE YOURSELVES"

Do not repay anyone evil for evil, but take thought for what is noble in the sight of all. If it is possible, so far as it depends on you, live peaceably with all. Beloved, never avenge yourselves, but leave room for the wrath of God; for it is written, "Vengeance is mine, I will repay, says the Lord." No, "if your enemies are hungry, feed them; if they are thirsty, give them something to drink; for by doing this you will heap burning coals on their heads." Do not be overcome by evil, but overcome evil with good. — Romans 12:17-21

In this passage, Paul instructs: "Do not repay anyone evil for evil" (Romans 12:17)—do not take revenge or try to balance the scales yourselves. If someone does something evil to you, do not repay that person with evil. Instead, when the evil person has a physical and basic need, meet that need in the hopes that your kindness will cause your enemy to repent.

"Beloved, never avenge *[ekdikéo]* yourselves" (Romans 12:19). *To avenge* means to bring justice. God says: "Vengeance is mine, I will repay" (Hebrews 10:30; see also Deuteronomy 32:35). In essence, He is saying, "Your enemy has caused you a great injustice, overwhelming loss, and pain; let Me bring you justice. I will not clear the guilty." God's vengeance is not vindictive—it is justice-making. He brings recompense, or awards compensation, to the sinned-against for the wrongs committed against them by their unrepentant offenders. Sometimes we think of God's wrath as the flip side of His love, but it is not. He is love and His love is eternal. His wrath is not. God's wrath is a disciplinary response to disobedience.

A young woman wanted so much to feel God's presence and to know His love, but all she could see was His anger. She believed her childhood sexual abuse trauma was her fault, and that God was going to "open the ground" as He did in the Old Testament and destroy her because He was angry with her.

Distortions about God's character are very normal for men and women who have been sinned against. Oftentimes, they are afraid of God because they see Him as angry and mean—unable to be pleased, and ready to punish them for sins that are not their own. I explained to this woman that God is love and will always be love. When that love was betrayed because Israel broke its covenantal promises to God, His wrath was a disciplinary response.

God's love is eternal; His discipline is temporary. When we get to heaven, God's love will be present, not His wrath or discipline. I also told her that her abuser sinned against her, and that God would hold this person accountable for that sin. His wrath would bring justice on her behalf by holding her abuser accountable for his sin against her. As I spoke these words, the Holy Spirit opened her heart to the truth of a loving God whose anger is kindled against sin and injustice.

We are created in the image of God to desire justice, and when we are denied this, we instantly know it. The sinned-against must *never* avenge themselves by taking justice into their own hands for the sins that have been committed against them. Many people seek to do this by making others pay—or making themselves pay—because their cries for justice demand it. God is not denying that there is a debt owed; instead, He is saying, "Let me handle the debt for you." He has taken to Himself the task of avenging the wronged and the sinned-against—those who have had evil deeds inflicted upon them. They are not to take justice into their own hands, but to leave room for God's vengeance. If the debt were not important to God, there would be no need for Him to avenge the sin.

The "prayer posture" for the sinned-against who have no chance of reconciliation and justice interpersonally, is to transfer the debts owed them to God—essentially, taking them out of their internal courts and appealing to the heavenly court for justice. Their unrepentant offender may become an enemy and must not be treated with the same evil. However, each one of us is commanded by God to overcome that person and "evil" with kindness. Our enemy can be someone who has not repented and is hostile, causing us pain, or setting traps for us. Sadly, our enemy may even be a family member.

"Love Your Enemy Into Repentance"

Paul echoes Jesus' teaching regarding the treatment of enemies (Matthew 5:43-48; Luke 6:27-36). We are to love *(agapáo)* our enemies with the same love our heavenly Father loves His enemies—with kindness. This love is mature and merciful, and even loves those who hate us with the goal of guiding our enemies into repentance. It is also the kind of love that prays for our enemies and gives a different response than the one expected—a blessing instead of cursing, peacemaking instead of violence, giving without expecting repayment for asking, and being kind instead of doing more evil. We win our enemies over with kindness. Our loving kindness—to love as the Lord loves—does not forgive them. Rather, it is meant to lead them to repentance and forgiveness—to transform them from enemy to friend. This kindness is expressed by taking care of a physical need, as made apparent by the Holy Spirit.

Paul further adds: "No, if your enemies are hungry, feed them . . . thirsty, give them something to drink . . . by doing this you will heap burning coals upon their heads" (Romans 12:20). When presented with an opportunity to do good to people who have harmed us, God wants us to take the opportunity that He has given. "If you see the donkey of someone who hates you fallen down under its load, do not leave it there; be sure you help him with it" (Exodus 23:5, NIV). Deeds of love also overcome evil. *Hungry* and *thirsty* give the idea of "continuously feeding him— morseling him—a little bit at a time—like a baby." The idea of feeding a baby or giving a baby a drink—holding the cup to the mouth—represents an act of loving kindness. You're not throwing the food or water at them. It is an active, relational act that is meant to bring your enemy to repentance.

Our enemy expects retaliation, and when we do something good to him, like give him something to eat or drink, or help his donkey, it heaps: "burning coals on his head" (Romans 12:20, NIV). This idiom has a couple of meanings. First, there is an Arab saying, "burning coals on the head and fire in the liver." It means that an enemy can deal with the fact that you hate him or her and is expecting evil for evil. However, he cannot deal with the fact that you are doing something nice for him. It may make them feel a burning sense of shame. Another view held by William Klassen points to an Egyptian custom in which a penitent person carries coals of fire in a bowl on his head, which is a dynamic symbol of a change of mind and repentance. Another view refers to the fact that in Bible times, coals were needed to keep the fire going, and carrying a container of hot coals on one's head would lead to a softening of the heart and ultimately to repentance. Each meaning has the same result. Loving kindness to our enemy may lead them to repentance.

OVERWHELMING KINDNESS

After Bill and I—along with our German shepherd named Gandalf—moved into a neighborhood in Point Hueneme, California, we discovered we had a neighbor who was hard to get to know. His wife was sweet and their kids were cute, but whenever we spoke to him, he rarely responded. While we didn't know much about one another, they knew we were Christians and attended church.

For some strange reason, whenever our dog would get out of our yard, he would head straight into theirs. Once, when Bill realized Gandalf was missing, he went to look for him and found Gandalf standing in their garage—but he wasn't alone. The man was holding him by the scruff of his neck with one hand, and held a knife in the other hand. From Bill's perspective, it appeared that he was moments away from harming our dog.

Our neighbor quickly became the enemy. Bill, angry over the man's extreme reaction, grabbed the dog and headed home, where he related the story to me. I felt a sense of hurt welling up from deep within me as I realized that if my husband had not shown up when he did, our neighbor would have hurt Gandalf. The worst part was the fact that we lived across the street from him, and saw the family every day.

Bill and I both realized that God could have a greater plan in mind for our circumstances. Therefore, we began to pray and ask the Lord to show us what He wanted us to do. This is when I received a strong impression to buy some flowers for their garden. This would have seemed like a strange suggestion had I not learned years ago to take God at His word. If He says, "Do good to those who hate you" (Luke 6:27), then I want to be obedient. Therefore, one day, I asked my husband, "What do you think about buying some plants for their garden?" An instant smile washed across his face, and I quickly countered, "No, not poisonous plants."

Bill did not warm up to the idea right away, so we waited. Many times, the Lord will press us to do something kind to those who we consider our enemies. Finally, my husband agreed to the flower idea, and we bought plants for their garden and attached a card to one of the pots that said, "Sorry, things have gotten out of hand." They thanked us, but nothing changed. We did not become friends, but at least we were cordial.

Months later, their dog got out and was missing. Their little boys rang our doorbell. When we opened it, they looked up at us, explained their situation, and then asked, "Would you pray and ask God to help us find our dog?"

We said, "Sure." Then we prayed and went out to find their dog. The Holy Spirit helped us find that dog. He was hiding under a car on the other side of the highway, in the parking lot of the Seabee Base. When Bill reached to get him, the dog bit him. However, my husband scooped the little dog up and took him back to the neighbor's house. It was definitely one of those moments when the wall that had divided us came down, and they apologized for the way things had happened. We became friends and even began to socialize.

Bill was treated for the dog bite, and we did not ask them to reimburse us. Taking advantage of the opportunity to do good won an enemy. Life gives us tough relational situations, but Scripture always has a solution for the challenges we face. Scripture works, and God calls us to test its benefits. Yes, what we may have to do could be uncomfortable. We had to swallow our pride to find a good plant for their yard, and it interrupted our day to look for their dog, but the results far outweighed any awkwardness. We became good neighbors and co-hosted block parties for our street.

A willing heart to forgive invites repentance, but unless the offender repents, there can be no interpersonal reconciliation. The wrongdoing becomes unforgivable. In the absence of forgiveness and reconciliation, we must take advantage of any opportunities God brings our way to love our enemies into repentance by our acts of kindness. Vertically in prayer, we are commanded to pray for our enemies and revoke our right for personal vengeance in light of God's expected avenging of the wrong.[23] Interpersonally, we are to look for opportunities to do good for them, with the hopes of turning an enemy into a friend. However, we are never commanded to forgive them interpersonally unless they repent. Until they do, we must continue to stand praying with that same believing prayer that can move mountains, and we must also "live peaceably with all" (Romans 12:18), so far as it depends on us, because our kindness may lead them to repentance.

> *In the absence of forgiveness and reconciliation, we must take advantage of any opportunities God brings our way to love our enemies into repentance by our acts of kindness.*

STEPS FOR REVOKING REVENGE

The concept of revoking our right to get even comes from a biblical worldview that understands that the sinned-against has the debt, the power, and the right for justice. If justice cannot be received in our interpersonal relationships because the offender is unwilling to repent, has never repented, or is unable to repent, the debt owed needs to be transferred to our avenging God. The sinned-against must be careful not to exact payment from anyone other than the one who sinned against them. They cannot make themselves or other people pay for wounds they never inflicted.

Forgiveness in this dimension is a three phase process of 1) remembering and mourning; 2) holding the offender responsible;

and 3) revoking revenge by transferring the debts owed to us and allowing God to avenge. This is not a religious exercise; it is the power and presence of the Holy Spirit helping the sinned-against to release the pain to God and to trust that the timing is in His hands.

For childhood abuse trauma, the process in the vertical dimension consists of five phases: 1) finding safety; 2) remembering and mourning; 3) holding the offender responsible; 4) revoking revenge; and 5) reconnecting with God and self. In a subsequent book, I will address the process of healing and transformation for childhood sexual abuse trauma in the VIP's (victor in process) relationship with God, self, and others.

Righteous and unrighteous anger

Revoking revenge begins with the awareness that the sinned-against has a right for justice. The initial cry for justice is a righteous anger that says, "This is wrong!" It is a righteous anger that rises up when we are the victims of an injustice. Righteous anger is not sin; it is a powerful motivator for change. However, when that cry for justice is muted, the righteous anger can become unrighteous anger that turns inward as bitterness, self-hatred, and shame—or it turns outward as rage that explodes onto others.

Righteous anger rises up against the injustice and fights to bring change. For example, Jesus overturned the moneychangers' tables in the temple (Matthew 21:12-16; Mark 11:15-18; Luke 19:45-47; John 2:14-16). His anger was directed at the men who made the court of the Gentiles into a marketplace filled with money-changers and animals for sale, leaving no room for the Gentiles to pray. That angered Jesus, and He took up a whip, overturned their tables, and drove them out saying: "Is it not written, 'My house shall be called a house of prayer for all the nations'?" (Mark 11:17). His anger was not sin; it was a righteous cry for justice, followed with a powerful action.

Not all anger is sin because we can be angry and not sin (Ephesians 4:26). Expressing anger is difficult for many believers because they believe that all anger is sinful. However, righteous cries for justice that come out in anger are not all sin. In fact, when handled in the right way and in the right setting, anger can prove to be a powerful emotion that can bring about the necessary changes. Bottled up anger can come out in a righteous way or in an unrighteous manner.

You can throw rocks at the ocean to get your anger out—you just cannot throw rocks at others. Finding safe and righteous ways to release your anger is an important part of the process of revoking revenge. Anger can be misdirected. For example, instead of being angry with the person who harmed you—because they are unavailable or unwilling to repent—you become angry with everyone and everything else. Unrighteous anger tries to balance the scale by making the wrong people pay the debt.

Remembering and mourning

There is a cry of the heart waiting to be heard. Grief work is something that helps the sinned-against find his or her voice and begin to identify the debts and subsequent losses that the wounding has caused. This heart-cry connects the losses with the emotion. We cannot go back and change the past. Cruel parents abused—and that cannot be changed in the mind of the adult believer who wants to be free from his or her captivity to the pain. Instead, he or she must remember and mourn the losses and put the blame where it belongs. Sometimes, however, the adult will create an idealized family in his or her mind that keeps the truth hidden. This process of remembering and mourning joins with the Holy Spirit to bring healing. Not all things have to be remembered. The Spirit has a view from within. He has been interceding on this person's behalf and will bring forth what is necessary for healing.

During this season of grief, usually the person cries out authentically before God, asks the tough questions of God, and seeks the comfort of another person who can bear witness to their pain. How long the season lasts is as individual as the wounding. Some people are able to get in touch with their emotions and losses, grieve them out, and it is done. Others are afraid of the pain because they have spent their lives keeping the pain sealed away and do not know how to articulate it. They are afraid they will lose their minds or get lost in a "black hole."

If you are afraid of emotion, it may be difficult for you to walk alongside someone who is grieving over his or her broken heart because you may want to calm it down too soon. It is important that you cooperate with the Holy Spirit—who is committed to meeting the person in the ashes of their lives, is interceding for their freedom, and is providing release to their cries for justice. The sinned-against need a witness—someone to hear their stories and someone who is willing to mourn with them (Romans 12:15). If possible, it should be a community grief because when the community bears witness to people's injustice and echoes their cries, the stage is set for a tremendous amount of healing to take place.

"As God is your witness"

Only God knows the undistorted truth of what happened during those painful, traumatic times of wounding in our lives. He is the only One who knows the perpetrator and what really happened. The sinned-against do not have to remember and mourn everything that happened in order to release their debts.

As God is our witness, He will hold the sinner accountable for everything. Therefore, when traumatic issues mute our voices, the Holy Spirit hears our cries. When distressing issues dissociate the events from our memories, He remembers and will not forget. God Himself—who is the only true witness to the sin and the crime in many cases—will hold the sinner accountable. Therefore, it is comforting to know that He will bear witness on our behalf in those cases awaiting justice.

Holding the offender responsible

In this phase of transferring the debt, the sinned-against must come to an understanding that the sinner is responsible for the wounding. They are also responsible for their sinful reactions to the wounds and must confess those reactions. However, abused and neglected children are not culpable—deserving blame or punishment—in the abuse, and must not be made to repent for the sin of abuse because it is not their sin. God will not hold them responsible for this sin. The victim of evil is not responsible for the evil inflicted. All forms of child abuse and neglect are evil. They are not merely dysfunctional; they are sinful and evil.

It is natural for little children who have been abused to see themselves as evil or bad because it is their way of staying connected or attached to abusive parents or caregivers. They will say, "I have good parents. If I can just be better, Dad or Mom will not hurt me." Unless they repent horizontally and vertically, God holds the abusing adults accountable.

Offenders offend. Sinners sin and must be held responsible by the victims of their sin in order for the sinned-against to transfer the debts owed. They will not transfer the debt if they believe they are responsible for the sins committed against them. Confessing sins that are not your sins does nothing to bring release—it only adds to the sense of injustice.

Revoking revenge

In this phase, the sinned-against voluntarily release their rights to take justice into their own hands and give the task to God, who has promised to avenge. It is in this phase that the sinned-against voice their stories and pain, and grieve before God and another person. This is where they pray, "Lord, please hold my debts; be my Avenger. I release **B**'s debt into your hands. I no longer want to make others pay for **B**'s debt—nor do I want to make myself pay. Also, please forgive me for turning to drugs or anything else in order to numb my pain." The sinned-against must be empowered with the choice and the voice to speak out and know that someone cares and someone is listening.

Prayers to revoke revenge are not simple. They involve the deepest cries of people's hearts and expressions of anger, hurt, and pain.

Through revoking revenge, a sense of power will be restored. God will hold the offender accountable. The wrongdoing is not undone or erased—it remains with the offender and God who will not clear the guilty. Instead, the offender remains subject to the consequences of his or her sins and crimes. If the offender repents to God for that sin, God will say: "Go and be reconciled with the one you sinned against. Then come back and offer your gift to Me." The offender always has to take step one before receiving God's forgiveness.

Prayers to revoke revenge are not simple. They involve the deepest cries of people's hearts and expressions of anger, hurt, and pain. Again, admitting our fears and frustrations before God gives voice to those deepest cries that were muted long ago.

Figure 7: Revoking Revenge for the Sinned-Against Illustrated

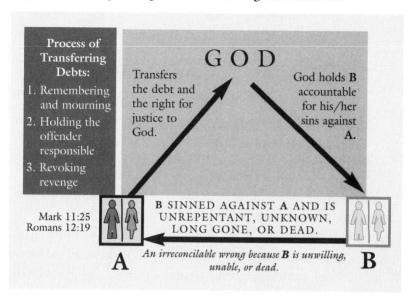

The revoking revenge model is illustrated in Figure 7 for those irreconcilable wrongs that cry out for justice in our hearts. The sinned-against can do nothing interpersonally. He can only vertically transfer the debt owed him out of their internal courts to the heavenly court Judge—who will hold the offenders responsible for those sins.

Repentance is not the way of release. He cannot repent for someone else's sin. Forgiving unrepentant people does not bring freedom either. Giving up our right to balance the scales (which we long to balance) by transferring those debts to our justice-making God for His righteous judgment, will bring a release to our hearts, minds, and spirits.

Hindrances to revoking revenge

Often, the sinned-against have distorted images of God, self, and others. When their cries for justice become muted and their anger turns unrighteous, they may not believe in an avenging, justice-making God, because He did not rescue them from their pain when it was first inflicted. Therefore, they may find it difficult to trust Him. This is the reality they live with, and God wants to meet them there.

The sinned-against may be afraid to trust Him with their debts and be hesitant to pray prayers that revoke their revenge. These distortions do not keep God from moving in their lives through His empowering Spirit. Yet, they must eventually acknowledge their distortions before God, "Lord, I want to trust You; but I am afraid and I am hurt that You did not help me when I needed You!" This admission brings freedom. Denying the distortions, or pretending that we do not feel that way, just keeps us stuck.

Sinned-against issues come up very frequently in conference, retreat, and church settings. Many times people are told they have to forgive no matter what; otherwise, they are in sin and the bitterness will affect them physically and spiritually. The typical response is, "OK, I'll keep trying to do it!"

Once, when my husband Bill was praying for a young man who had been physically and emotionally abused by his father, he told him, "It wasn't your sin—it was your father's sin. It's your father who needs to repent to you and to God." The man broke and cried in his arms. He said, "I always blamed myself and believed that I was in sin. It was my fault my father hit me. It was my fault that my father got drunk. It was my fault because I was not a good son! And it is my fault that I am having a hard time forgiving him!"

Bill explained that he was sinned against and that God heard the cry for justice from his heart. He also prayed that the man would be able to release his father to God, and that God would bring justice to the situation. The young man was ready to do that. If his father ever came to repent, he said he would be ready to forgive. He would begin to pray for such an encounter to take place because his father was still in his life.

ten

A Two-Step, Two Dimensional Guide to Forgiveness

As we have seen, biblical forgiveness is not unilateral. It is a two-step process that affects our personal relationship with God and our interpersonal relationships—whether they are with believers, non-believers, or with someone who is considered an enemy. When **B** sins against **A**, what happens next will depend upon what **A** and **B** do in their relationship with one another. In this chapter, I will demonstrate how a two-step, two-dimensional model will help identify the steps for **A** and for **B** to follow, and what to do when the reconciliation process breaks down.

However, two important points must be made before we proceed. First, the circle of a person's sin is the circle of his or her confession. In other words, only the people involved in the circle of sin are involved in the confession, repentance, and forgiveness. Second, there is no "third party forgiveness," in which a person outside the circle repents to the sinned-against on behalf of the sinner.

THE CIRCLE OF SIN

If I sin against God alone—such as with evil thoughts, sexual fantasies, or idolatry of the heart—then my sin is between God and me. I must repent for my sin to God, demonstrating my fruit of repentance by doing deeds that change my behaviors. For example, if I repented for viewing pornography on the Web, I may have to cancel my Internet service so that I will not be tempted to sin in the same way.

If I sin against someone else, I must first go to that person, repent, be reconciled, and then ask God to forgive me for that sin. A sin against another is a sin against God. Whoever is in the circle must be involved in the reconciliation process. When I sin against others, God is always included in the circle. If I sin against more than one person at the same time, they must all be involved in my repentance before I can ask God to forgive my sin. The circle of sin is the circle of confession, repentance, and forgiveness.

Case Study: Figure 8 illustrates a story between **A, B, C,** and **D** who all attend the same church. **A** is having a difficult time in his marriage, and because of the added job pressure, he decides to step down as worship team leader for now. His absence is noticed, and his reasons for stepping down are unknown to everyone except the pastor. **B** knows **A** and is aware of his personal struggles. **B** sins against **A** by gossiping to **C** about the "real" reasons he stepped down from ministry when **C** asked, "I wonder what happened to **B**?" **C** then tells **D** under the disguise of prayer, and the cycle ends with **D**. **A** wonders why **C** says one day, "I'm praying for you."

Figure 8: Gossip and the Circle of Sin

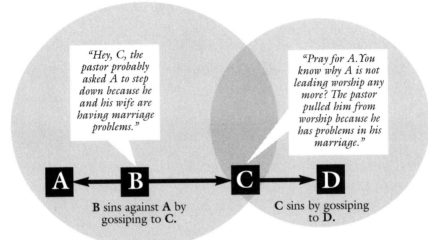

Gossip can be a complex sin to confront and mediate. Who is in **B**'s circle? Everyone that **B** involved in the sin is within his circle—**A** and **C**, too. Who is in **C**'s circle? Everyone that **C** involved in the sin of gossip, as well as **D**. Here are the steps to forgiveness for **A**, **B**, **C**, and **D**.

A	B	C	D
Step One: Receive a repentant **B** and be willing to forgive. That includes proof of **B**'s repentance by clearing **A**'s name to **C**. Receive a repentant **C** and be willing to forgive. That includes proof of **C**'s repentance by clearing **A**'s name to **D**.	**Step One:** Go and repent to **A** and receive **A**'s forgiveness. Also, go repent to **C** and clear **A**'s name (Matthew 5:23-24). **Step Two:** Ask God to forgive the sin of gossip.	**Step One:** Receive a repentant **B** and repent to **B** for participating in the gossip. Also, go and repent to **D** and clear **A**'s name. **Step Two:** Ask God to forgive the sin of gossip.	**Step One:** Receive a repentant **C**, who clears **A**'s name

NO THIRD PARTY FORGIVENESS

Third party forgiveness is a psychological technique used to help the sinned-against forgive an unrepentant offender. This method uses a substitute in the place of the offender in an effort to release the sinned-against from his or her captivity to the hurtful event. The goal of third party forgiveness is to help the sinned-against find freedom through unilateral forgiveness. For example, if a woman was sexually abused by her father when she was a child, another man would stand in his place and say, "Please forgive me for abusing you as a little girl. I hurt you. I was wrong." Unilaterally, the woman would be encouraged to forgive her father through this man who is standing in the place of her father. Often, people tell me how pressured they felt at that moment to say, "I forgive you." They believed that if they did not forgive the other party, God would not forgive their sins or heal their wounds.

The problem with third party forgiveness is three-fold.

• *First, the offender—her father—owes her the debt and is the only one who must take responsibility for that sin.*

• *Second, it minimizes the sinned-against's wounding by offering words without repentance, by someone not engaged interpersonally at all.* This stand-in for the father may be compassionately moved by the captivity of the woman to her past pain, but having her unilaterally forgive a "repentant father-figure"—in place of her unrepentant father—cheapens her loss.

• *Third, the third party is outside the circle of sin, as Figure 9 illustrates.*

We all know times when the Holy Spirit bears witness to our efforts to bring healing to the sinned-against—even using third party forgiveness—and the person feels a sense of release. That is the grace of God covering our well-meaning efforts. More often, third party forgiveness brings only a temporary release, because the interpersonal transaction is incomplete without the real repentant father owning up to the debt. People respond to the moment, but biblical forgiveness is more than a momentary release.

Figure 9: No Third Party Forgiveness

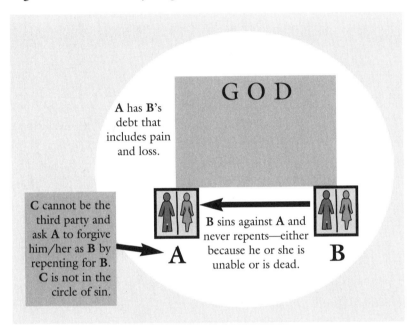

Helping her revoke her right to justice and transferring the debt she is owed to God, validates her pain, gives her a voice, and brings the release she needs and desires. She puts her trust in an avenging God—who will put godly pressure on her father to repent if he is still alive; or who will be his Judge if he is dead.

Compassionate solidarity and advocacy from the father-figure—who is standing with her in her suffering and echoing her cries for justice before God—will bring her greater comfort than if he pretends to fulfill the obligation of her real father. His support says to her, "Someone hears my voice, sees my pain, bears witness to my losses, and agrees that what my father did to me was sin—and a crime!"

ASSESSING THE DEBT OWED

When **B** sins against **A**, **B** is indebted to **A**, and only **A** can assess the debt owed. The sinned-against must assess what is owed before the issue can be resolved. The challenge for **A** is not to minimize the debt or pain by saying, "Oh, it's okay, I forgive you." Additionally, **A** must not to add the pain to other irreconcilable offenses, making it almost impossible to win the other because the two parties cannot come to agreement.

Case Study (Figure 10): Believer **B** sins against **A** by lying, and **A** becomes angry, hurt, and explosive. However, **A** has had a long history of people sinning against her by lying. **C** lied to **A**, **D** and **E** lied as well. Neither **C**, **D**, nor **E** has ever repented to **A**. **B**'s debt is now combined with previous wounds. **B** does not understand the reason there is so much emotional stress over the lie he told.

Figure 10: Sorting Out the Debt

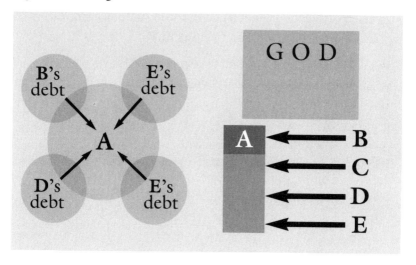

If **B** wants to reconcile with **A**, someone must help **A** to assess the debt. It is important that **A** understands what part of her pain belongs to **B**'s lying and what part of her pain is the result of others lying to her. **A** must assess **B**'s true debt for this incident and not make **B** pay for **C**, **D**, and **E**. She may be unaware that she is making others pay. That is part of the process of healing. **B** can come and ask her to forgive him for lying and demonstrate fruit of repentance by becoming a truth-teller (Ephesians 4:25). However, **B** must not be held accountable for sin that he did not commit. **A** may be expecting **B** to pay the full debt—$5000— when in reality **B**'s debt is only $500. Once the true debt is established, **B** can repent for what he has done, **A** can forgive, and they can be reconciled. Part of **A**'s healing is grieving out the losses of **C**, **D**, and **E** by revoking her right for revenge and transferring those debts to God. It may also involve confronting **C**, **D**, and **E**—this may be the next step in **A**'s healing and release. It also raises the question of why are people lying to **A**.

Counseling involves helping **A** and **B** sort out what is owed so that repentance, forgiveness, and reconciliation can happen in their relationship. It may also involve helping **A** process through the revoking revenge prayer model to grieve out the losses of **C**, **D**, and **E**'s wounding, so that **A** can find freedom and healing— thereby improving **A**'s relationship with **B**.

Confronting an Unbeliever

We cannot hold unbelievers to Scripture, nor can the church take disciplinary action against them when they are unwilling to repent. Unbelievers are judged because of their rejection of Christ and their unwillingness to repent vertically. They stand under God's judgment. However, the biblical principles of interpersonal repentance and forgiveness do hold true. Much like the Twelve

Steps—which are biblical principles that are being applied in secular groups—these biblical principles can be applied with unbelieving family members, friends, neighbors, etc.

As believers, we are commanded to pray to God and forgive them (Mark 11:25), and to release our right to revenge (Romans 12:19). These steps prepare our hearts to move forward in life. If a family member sins against us, we can follow the biblical principles of going privately to him or her first. If we can't work it out,

As believers, we are commanded to pray to God and forgive them, and to release our right to revenge.

we must find someone to mediate the situation—someone the offender listens to and respects.

If this still doesn't work, you can withhold your relationship or create new, limited boundaries in which you are willing to interact with this person. Again, it's not about pretending everything is fine—it's about working things out peacefully. Certainly, we all understand how family tension spreads, but family peace can spread in the same manner. It's not easy, but we are not alone. We have the Holy Spirit, who may use this situation to bring that family member to salvation. Therefore, if we are ever going to see families changed for the better, we must be willing to engage in the tough issues.

UNSAFE PEOPLE TO CONFRONT

Family members and other people who have inflicted evil upon you through childhood sexual abuse, ritual abuse, or physical and verbal abuse, and have not repented, may be unsafe to confront. You can take the prayer posture (Mark 11:25), and seek God regarding what to do in this situation. Again, transferring the debt to God will help you find a release of the pain as you grieve out those losses before an avenging God. I have heard too many stories over the years of people who have unilaterally forgiven their abusing parents, and have gone home only to be abused again. I would recommend that you talk to your counselor before confronting such people.

STEPS TO FORGIVENESS IN TWO DIMENSIONS OF RELATIONSHIP

The chart in Figure 11 illustrates the steps to forgiveness in our vertical relationship with God and our interpersonal relationships. This chart summarizes the steps to take if we have sinned against others, or if we have been sinned against, by another believer, a non-believer, or even an enemy.

Figure 11: Steps to Forgiveness

If I sin against others:	If I have been sinned against by another believer:	If I have been sinned against by a non-believer:	If I have been sinned against by an enemy:	If I have been sinned against by someone who I am unable to confront:
Matthew 5:24 "Go; first be reconciled."	Mark 11:25 "Stand praying, forgive . . . anything against anyone." Romans 12:19 "Vengeance is mine."	Mark 11:25 "Stand praying, forgive . . . anything against anyone." Romans 12:19 "Vengeance is mine."	Mark 11:25 "Stand praying, forgive . . . anything against anyone." Romans 12:19 "Vengeance is mine."	Romans 12:19 "Vengeance is mine."
Step 1: Go and ask for forgiveness with true repentance—not only with words, but with actions and a heart that demonstrates that you want to change.	**Step 1:** Pray and release the debts owed you to God. Keep your door open for reconciliation so that your prayers will not be hindered.	**Step 1:** Pray and release the debts owed you to God. Keep your door open for reconciliation so that your prayers will not be hindered.	**Step 1:** Revoke your right to get justice—transfer debts to God. Keep your door open so that your prayers will not be hindered.	**Step 1:** Remember and mourn the losses. Hold the offender responsible, but transfer the debts owed you to God—for His justice in this age or the age to come.
Step 2: Ask God to forgive you for that sin. If you don't go, your prayers will be hindered because you will not be able to ask God to forgive you for that sin. The first step in asking God is asking the one you sinned against to forgive you and be reconciled.	**Step 2:** Luke 17:3 "Rebuke the offender." If that person repents and demonstrates fruit, forgive him or her. Give grace for the process of making that U-turn. If there is repentance, you must forgive. **IF NO REPENTANCE** Matthew 18:15-20 gives steps to reconciliation, but repentance is necessary before you can extend forgiveness. Your heart must want reconciliation and grieve over the lost one who refused to repent. Keep your door open.	**Step 2:** You can follow the biblical principles and go privately and confront. Forgive if there is repentance with demonstrated fruit of change. Give grace for the process of making that U-turn. **IF NO REPENTANCE** You can still follow the principles. Take someone with you as a witness, and if there is no repentance, withhold or create new, limited boundaries for your relationship. Keep your door open.	**Step 2:** When presented with an opportunity to do good, take it. Bring your enemy to repentance by not retaliating, and by doing the opposite of what is expected. You cannot forgive interpersonally until there is repentance. Keep your door open.	No Step 2

THE TRUTH BEHIND SELF-FORGIVENESS

Religious individualism believes that not only must we ask God to forgive our sins, we must also forgive ourselves for the sinful acts we commit. Self-forgiving may seem therapeutic, but is it really? Is it a horizontal confrontation with myself where I ask, "How could I do that?" Or is it a vertical process, which takes a god-like position that condemns the self and then forgives that same self? Scripture does not encourage us to forgive ourselves, but rather, to put our faith and trust in the forgiveness of God for our sins. It is,the washing away of our guilt so that we can approach God: "With a true heart in full assurance of faith, with our hearts sprinkled clean from an evil conscience and our bodies washed with pure water" (Hebrews 10:22). Forgiving self does not bring release. Instead, acknowledging our sinful self in light of the regenerated self brings a release in our hearts and minds.

Paul begins Ephesians with the incredible theology of a relational God, who lavishes every spiritual blessing upon us in Christ—through Christ and by Christ—according to His good pleasure and will. Our response to hearing the truth is to believe in the work of Christ and His sufficiency to cover all of our sins, as He draws us into an intimate relationship with our heavenly Father. We are His personally adopted sons and daughters.

Paul reminds the Ephesians: "You were dead through the trespasses and sins in which you once lived" (Ephesians 2:1-2). He then changes pronouns in Ephesians 2:3 and says: "All of us once lived among them in the passions of our flesh, following the desires of flesh and senses, and we were by nature children of wrath, like everyone else." Paul included himself, *"All of us once lived."*

Then he drives his point deep into our hearts: "But God, who is rich in mercy . . . even when we were dead through our trespasses made us alive together with Christ" (Ephesians 2:4-5). The power of "but God" transcends our sinful lifestyles before Christ, breaks the power of our sinful thought processes, and begins to work Christ in us through the indwelling presence of the Holy Spirit. When your accuser reminds you of your past sins ("You are not good enough for God! You committed adultery!"), do not fight to prove him wrong or endlessly try to forgive yourself. Instead, stand in the truth of God's infinite forgiveness as you reply, "Yes, I did commit adultery, *but God* has forgiven me, and raised me up, and seated me in heavenly places!" Forgiving self does nothing, because it is not within our power to do so. We know that. However, *receiving* God's forgiveness and standing in the wonderful provision of *but God* in our lives, agrees with what we once were—and yet sets our eyes on Whose we are and who we are becoming.

FINDING FREEDOM IN A FORGIVING GOD

To forgive another means to cancel the debt of what is owed in order to provide an open door for reconciliation. The sinner is indebted to the sinned-against. God will never sin, and has never sinned against anyone; and He certainly is indebted to no one. We must not encourage people to forgive God for letting them down, hurting them, failing to rescue them, or disappointing them. Again, that is merely a therapeutic approach to help the sinned-against find release.

> *The Book of Psalms is full of questions: How long? Where are you God? Have you forgotten us? We can give no answers that satisfy their why questions; only God can answer them—and He will.*

I believe that the sinned-against can express their disappointment to God, cry out from their place of confusion and hurt, and ask the tough "why" questions. The Book of Psalms is full of questions: How long? Where are you God? Have you forgotten us? We can give no answers that satisfy their why questions; only God can answer them—and He will. Helping them work through the disappointments and giving God an opportunity to meet them in their pain and answer these questions, is a far better approach. He is capable of answering every one of our tough questions. Therefore, we should never hesitate to bring our needs and sorrows to Him in prayer, and to encourage others to do so by our willingness to echo their cries.

IMPLICATIONS FOR LEADING PEOPLE TO CHRIST

New believers should be encouraged to make amends with those people they have harmed in their lives before they accepted Christ as their Savior. It is not a requirement for salvation, because we know that salvation is a gift that cannot be earned. However, the fruit of repentance validates the transforming power of the Holy Spirit in a person's life. A person who supports a unilateral approach would say, "When you give your life to Jesus, you become a new person in Christ and the old you has passed away" (2 Corinthians 5:17). This is true because it is the good news of the gospel. However, is Paul saying that the "old" does not have to be addressed any longer, and that the sins of the past can be forgotten because you are new now?

My question to this line of thinking is this: What about those "old" people you sinned against—the ones who are still healing from the wounds you inflicted before you were a Christian? Is there anybody that the Spirit is directing you to so that you can make amends—or go to, repent, and ask to be forgiven? Think about the witness it would be to the ones we've sinned against to hear us come back and say, "I've given my life to Christ and am changing who I am. Please forgive me for sinning against you, for abandoning you, abusing you, stealing from you, lying to you, and slandering you."

This is the type of action that exemplifies the power of repentance and forgiveness, and it is used to transform lives and bring others to Christ. I'm not saying that we must make amends to everyone we have ever harmed before we began our relationship with Christ. However, what I am saying is that we need to ask the Holy Spirit to make us sensitive to His leading and to bring to mind those whose forgiveness we need to seek. Then we need to be obedient.

Making amends as directed by the Holy Spirit can have a liberating effect in the lives of the sinned-against. Can you imagine what it would be like if you had experienced abuse as a child and the one who sinned against you came to Christ and wanted to repent to you and seek your forgiveness? Contemplate what it would be like if this same person were willing to say, "I know my sin against you has also caused you financial hardship, and I want to make restitution by helping you financially. I don't expect you to trust me, but I am willing to live within whatever boundaries you need in order to prove my repentance to you." Can you imagine what true repentance and forgiveness can do to begin the healing process in that relationship?

This happened to a woman I had been counseling. She had been sexually abused by her father as a little girl. He was a minister. She worked hard for years to find freedom from the devastating effects of the abuse in her life, and struggled hard to see God differently than her father. She found some freedom. Her father called her one day, and said that he had rededicated his life to Christ. He wanted to repent to her for the sins he had committed against her and the pain he had caused her all those years. She couldn't believe it! She forgave him over the phone because the door of her heart was open. She received a whole new dimension of freedom in both dimensions of relationship! Her father received the forgiveness he needed from his daughter, and could now ask God to forgive him. Once this took place, he could sense the Lord's forgiveness in his life. She cautiously began to reestablish their relationship. That's how it's supposed to work, I believe, for true repentance and forgiveness to heal our broken relationships.

However, we know it doesn't always work out this way. After Bill and I had become believers and were living for Jesus, we believed that God was directing us to return to Pennsylvania and repent to specific people we had sinned against. We repented to God for our sins and believed that God had forgiven us. Yet, He was also compelling us to go to two specific people and ask to be forgiven. Now, we are just baby believers—not even committed to a church family. I don't even believe we had been baptized yet. However, it was necessary in our thinking to drive 3,000 miles to find these people. Bill had to repent to one of them, and I had to repent to two. Now, we were scared, but I believe the Holy Spirit gave us the courage to go (and kept our car running along the way). I wish I could say we were well received, and that—as a result of our obedience—both people came to faith in Christ. That didn't happen. But what did happen was that we admitted our sins and had a humble attitude of repentance. Both Bill and I were willing to hear their anger and hurt. One forgave and one did not. The one who forgave eventually reconnected with us. We had to leave the one that did not in God's hands and to our door open when and if there is contact again. Our task was to be obedient and we were. We still do not know the outcome.

Looking back now, I can see God's grace and guidance in our lives as we took Him at His word to: "leave your gift . . . and go; first be reconciled" (Matthew 5:24). He moved our heart and our feet towards reconciliation to demonstrate that we were truly different, changing people, and that we were truly sorry for the sins we had committed in our ignorance and rebellion against God, because we hurt people we cared about.

If new believers "do deeds consistent with repentance" (Acts 26:20) through discipleship (that includes making amends to those people the Spirit reveals—maybe even including restitution), the gospel would become even more attractive to the lost— especially to the one awaiting the offender's repentance.

Furthermore, think of the rippling effect that could result as pastoral counselors prepare the hearts of the ones who were sinned against to receive a repentant offender. They could become an important part of the reconciliation process by helping the hurting people establish new boundaries for their mended relationships. Again, it's not about seeing everything through rose-colored glasses and asking the sinned-against to now welcome the sinner back as if there has been no wounding. The fruit of repentance must be demonstrated. The offender must be willing to live within the new boundaries—which may include "no relationship at this time." I believe the power of true repentance and forgiveness can mend the deepest relational wounds and bear witness to the transforming power of the gospel of Jesus Christ.

Epilogue

Wounds from others hurt our hearts, and, oftentimes, there is very little repentance or forgiveness. Because the church has had a predominantly unilateral view of forgiveness, many men and women have been encouraged to forgive unrepentant offenders for their own sake—to let themselves off the hook so that they will feel better. Too often, Scripture verses relating to the subject of forgiveness are strung together like pearls and become an overwhelming weight or millstone around the neck of the sinned-against.

Forgiving people who have never repented—through various methods and exercises—is an attempt to bring peace to the heart of the sinned-against. However, these methods are often viewed as unjust, and can be compared to adding salt to a wound. Well-meaning Christian counselors, pastors, and friends pressure the offended to forgive for their own good. They counsel them to let the offense go in order for God to forgive the offended of his or her own sins.

Furthermore, I believe countless people have become disillusioned and have left the church because of the sins that other believers have committed against them. Part of the problem lies with our unilateral teaching of repentance and forgiveness. As a result, people either do not tell one another about the problems facing them, or do not know how to ask someone to help them work things out with another believer. They keep trying to "let it go," but the hurt doesn't go. Rather, it is compounded with previous woundings and misunderstandings, and it affects their vertical relationship with God. Our churches must become safe, reconciling communities, where we teach our members reconciliation skills as part of the discipleship process, for the sake of maintaining community peace and the presence of God in our midst.

If you've been sinned against and are angry with God and the church, I want to encourage you to pour out your heart to God. Tell Him how you were hurt and what you lost as a result of someone's unrepentant sin against you. Transfer your debt to Him and let the Holy Spirit bring freedom to your heart—giving you the courage you need to return to church and take the proper steps to make things right. My prayer is that you will consider this book an attempt to leave the 99 other sheep in order to go and find you.

If you've been sinned-against, have only had unilateral forgiveness as your model, and have struggled trying to forgive an unrepentant offender, I want you to know that your voice is being heard. God wants you to pour out your heart to Him. He is on your side and will be your Avenger. Use the revoking revenge prayer model with a counselor or friend.

If the Holy Spirit is prompting your heart to repent to someone you have sinned against, please ask that person if you can come and repent. For some situations, it may be necessary to seek counsel as to how to approach the person you have harmed, because he or she may be untrusting or afraid. However, don't let that hinder your going, just guide it.

A couple of years ago, while I was teaching at a conference, a woman came up for prayer and asked me to pray that she would be able to forgive her husband for his sin of adultery. She said, "I keep trying to forgive him, but I still feel angry at him. I have been trying for the past year, and I can't. I don't want to be unforgiving, because I can't ask God to forgive me until I forgive him! Will you pray that I can forgive him?"

I said, "Can I ask you one question?"

She said, "Yes."

"Has your husband ever repented for his sin of adultery and breaking your covenant relationship?"

"No, he never has. As a matter of fact, the church has forgiven him, and he has since remarried. In fact, he is in the church, and I am out!"

"Yes, I'd love to pray for you. But first I'd like to explain something to you about forgiveness."

I took three minutes to explain the two dimensions of relationship, and how repentance and forgiveness are linked and operate on both levels. Then I shared with her that God is on the side of the sinned-against. She is owed a debt, and her responsibility is to transfer the debt that is owed her to the Lord for His justice. I encouraged her to take the case out of her internal court and transfer it to the heavenly court, and then to wait for God to either bring justice on her behalf, or to put godly pressure on her ex-husband to repent for his sins against her and make an attempt to ask for her forgiveness. Until then, he would still be held accountable for his sins against her. My task was to help her realize that she needed to transfer the debt and be ready to forgive him if he repented. She also needed to be prepared to confront him for his repentance.

By the time I concluded, her eyes were flooded with tears, and she said, "I've never heard it presented that way. I can do that!" We prayed, and she poured out her heart to God readily and easily transferred the debt to Him. She knew that she didn't have to pretend everything was fine in her relationship with her ex-husband. He still needed to repent to her and ask for her forgiveness. If he asked, she was willing to forgive him. She was willing to keep her door open. She left with new freedom, because she now knew that she was not in unforgiveness and could pray to God with a clear conscience.

She had rediscovered the power of repentance and forgiveness and was on the road to healing and new hope.

About the Author

For years in college classrooms and Christian conferences, Leah Coulter has helped people come to a true understanding of biblical repentance and forgiveness. She is a faculty member of The King's College and Seminary, Van Nuys, California; and an adjunct professor at Vineyard Leadership Institute, Columbus, Ohio, and Fuller Theological Seminary, Pasadena, California. She also is the author of A Pastoral Theology for the Sinned-Against: Adult Christian Women Sexually Abused as Children, appearing in the American Journal of Pastoral Counseling (Haworth Pastoral Press, 2001).

Leah received her master of divinity from Oral Roberts University, and her Ph.D. from Fuller Theological Seminary. She serves as Senior Associate Pastor of Channel Islands Vineyard Christian Fellowship in Oxnard, California, alongside her husband Bill.

If you would like to be on her mailing list for future conferences and upcoming publications, or would like a copy of her dissertation, "Pastoral Theology of Rescue and Relationship for the Sinned-Against: Solidarity and Empowerment for Christian Women Sexually Abused as Children," please visit her website: www.drleah.org or email her: info@drleah.org.

Chapter Two: The Pitfalls of Religious Individualism

[1]David W. Augsburger, *Helping People Forgive*, (Louisville, KY: Westminster John Knox Press, 1996).

[2]Robert N. Bellah, Richard Madsen, William M. Sullivan, Ann Swidler, and Steven M. Tipton, *Habits of the Heart, Individualism and Commitment in American Life*, (New York, NY: Harper & Row, Publishers, 1985).

[3]Julie A. Gorman, *Community That Is Christian, A Handbook on Small Groups*, (Wheaton, ILL: Victor Books, 1993).

[4]David W. Augsburger, *Helping People Forgive*, (Louisville, KY: Westminster John Knox Press, 1996).

[5]Gregory L. Jones, *Embodying Forgiveness*, (Grand Rapids, MI: William B. Eerdmans Publishing Company, 1995).

[6]C. Norman Kraus, *The Community of the Spirit, How the Church Is in the World*, (Scottdale, PA: Herald Press, 1993).

Chapter Three: Understanding the Two Dimensions of Relationship

[7]Walter A. Elwell, Editor, *Evangelical Dictionary of Biblical Theology*, (Grand Rapids, MI: Baker Books, 2000).

[8]C. Norman Kraus, *The Community of the Spirit, How the Church Is in the World*, (Scottdale, PA: Herald Press, 1993).

[9]W. Arndt, F.W. Gingrich, F.W. Danker, & W. Bauer, *A Greek-English Lexicon of the New Testament and Other Early Christian Literature*, (Chicago: University of Chicago Press, 1996, c1979).

[10]C.F. Keil & F. Delitzsch, *Commentary on the Old Testament*. (Oak Harbor, WA: Logos Research Systems, Inc., 2002).

[11]John E. Hartley, *Word Biblical Commentary, Leviticus*, (Dallas, TX: Word Books, Publisher, 1992), 317.

Chapter Four: Forgiving as the Lord Forgives

[12]K. S. Wuest, *Wuest's Word Studies From the Greek New Testament: For the English Reader*. (Grand Rapids: Eerdmans, 1997, c1984).

[13]Johannes P. Louw and Eugene A. Nida, *Greek-English Lexicon of the New Testament Based on Semantic Domains*, (New York: United Bible Societies, 1989).

Chapter Five: Learning to Forgive in Two Dimensions

[14]Geoffrey W. Bromiley, *Theological Dictionary of the New Testament*, (Grand Rapids, MI: William B. Eerdmans Publishing Company, Vol. 1, 1985), 509.

[15]Johannes P. Louw and Eugene A. Nida, *Greek-English Lexicon of the New Testament Based on Semantic Domains*, (New York: United Bible Societies, 1989).

Chapter Seven: Forgiveness in Your Relationship With God

[16]William Klassen, *The Forgiving Community*, (Philadelphia, PA: Westminster Press, 1966).

[17]Colin Brown, Editor, *The New International Dictionary of New Testament Theology, Vol. 3*, (Grand Rapids, MI: Zondervan Publishing House 1986), 585-586.

[18]Howard I Marshall, *New International Greek Testament Commentary*, (Grand Rapids, MI: William B. Eerdmans Publishing Co., 1978).

[19]Wendell E. Miller, *Forgiveness, The Power and The Puzzle*, (Warsaw, IN: ClearBrook Publishers, 1994), 106.

Chapter Eight: Interpersonal Forgiveness for the Sinner and the Sinned-Against

[20]Fritz Rienecker and Cleon Rogers, *Linguistic Key to the Greek New Testament*. (Grand Rapids, MI: Zondervan Publishing House, 1980).

[21]Howard I. Marshall, *New International Greek Testament Commentary, Commentary on Luke*. (Grand Rapids, MI: William B. Eerdmans Publishing Co., 1978), 642.

Chapter Nine: Revoking Revenge and Justice for the Sinned-Against

[22]Robertson, A. 1997. *Word Pictures in the New Testament.* Vol.V c1932, Vol.VI c1933 by Sunday School Board of the Southern Baptist Convention. (Oak Harbor, WA: Logos Research Systems, Inc. 2002).

[23]John Nolland, *Luke 18:35-24:53, Word Biblical Commentary, Vol. 35c,* (Dallas, TX: Word Books, 1993), 838.

Figures:

1. Loving God, our Neighbors, and our Enemies

2. Ten Commandments' Vertical & Horizontal Relational Laws

3. Sinner Indebted to Sinned-Against

4. Vertical Step to Prepare Our Hearts

5. Two-Step Process for the Sinner

6. A Two-Step, Two-Dimensional Process for Sinner and Sinned-Against

7. Revoking Revenge for the Sinned-Against Illustrated

8. Gossip and the Circle of Sin

9. No Third Party Forgiveness

10. Sorting Out the Debt

11. Steps to Forgiveness

Revolutionary Leadership
by Tri Robinson
Retail price: $12.95

Is your church growing? More importantly, is your church creating authentic followers of Jesus? In *Revolutionary Leadership*, author and pastor Tri Robinson shares his journey of planting a church that is serious about discipleship. Out of his desire to pastor a church that was intentional and successful at developing passionate followers of Jesus, Robinson discovered the concept of synergy and how its components can help revolutionize leadership within a church.

Sample chapters and book are available for purchase at: www.ampelonpublishing.com

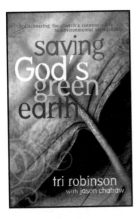

Saving God's Green Earth
by Tri Robinson
Retail price: $12.95

For hundreds of years, the church championed the beauty of God's creation, demonstrating in many ways how it points to the Creator. However, over the last century, the evangelical church has let the value of caring for creation slip away. Author and pastor Tri Robinson makes a compelling case for the biblical mandate behind environmental stewardship and shows the church what it can do about this eroding value.

Not only does Robinson inspire the reader to care for the environment, he reveals a clear pathway to making the value of environmental stewardship real in both the life of the reader and the Christian community in which he or she is involved.